ISBN 0-8373-0095-9

C-95   CAREER EXAMINATION SERIES

D1465927

This is your
PASSBOOK® for...

Bridge
& Tunnel
Officer

Test Preparation Study Guide

Questions & Answers

NLC
NATIONAL LEARNING CORPORATION

Copyright © 2003 by

National Learning Corporation

212 Michael Drive, Syosset, New York 11791

(516) 921-8888
Outside N.Y.: 1(800) 645-6337
ORDER FAX: 1(516) 921-8743
www.passbooks.com
email: passbooks @ aol.com

PRINTED IN THE UNITED STATES OF AMERICA

PASSBOOK®

NOTICE

PASSBOOK SERIES®

THE *PASSBOOK SERIES*® has been created to prepare applicants and candidates for the ultimate academic battlefield—the examination room.

At some time in our lives, each and every one of us may be required to take an examination—for validation, matriculation, admission, qualification, registration, certification, or licensure.

Based on the assumption that every applicant or candidate has met the basic formal educational standards, has taken the required number of courses, and read the necessary texts, the *PASSBOOK SERIES*® furnishes the one special preparation which may assure passing with confidence, instead of failing with insecurity. Examination questions—together with answers—are furnished as the basic vehicle for study so that the mysteries of the examination and its compounding difficulties may be eliminated or diminished by a sure method.

This book is meant to help you pass your examination provided that you qualify and are serious in your objective.

The entire field is reviewed through the huge store of content information which is succinctly presented through a provocative and challenging approach—the question-and-answer method.

A climate of success is established by furnishing the correct answers at the end of each test.

You soon learn to recognize types of questions, forms of questions, and patterns of questioning. You may even begin to anticipate expected outcomes.

You perceive that many questions are repeated or adapted so that you gain acute insights, which may enable you to score many sure points.

You learn how to confront new questions, or types of questions, and to attack them confidently and work out the correct answers.

You note objectives and emphases, and recognize pitfalls and dangers, so that you may make positive educational adjustments.

Moreover, you are kept fully informed in relation to new concepts, methods, practices, and directions in the field.

You discover that you are actually taking the examination all the time: you are preparing for the examination by "taking" an examination, not by reading extraneous and/or supererogatory textbooks.

In short, this PASSBOOK®, used directedly, should be an important factor in helping you to pass your test.

BRIDGE AND TUNNEL OFFICER

WHAT THE JOB INVOLVES: Bridge And Tunnel Officers (BTOs) perform various duties concerned with vehicular traffic on the bridge and tunnel facilities of the Triborough Bridge and Tunnel Authority (an agency of the Metropolitan Transportation Authority) in New York City. BTOs collect tolls; resolve problems in E-Z Pass traffic lanes; interact with customers and provide assistance, such as giving travel directions and traffic information; help stranded motorists; direct traffic and clear traffic lanes on bridges, in tunnels, and on toll plazas; patrol structures and roadways; drive various types of motor vehicles; complete forms and reports; respond to traffic emergencies and administer first aid to injured motorists. BTOs issue summonses, make arrests and perform other law enforcement functions, such as testifying in court or at administrative hearings, and communicating with law enforcement officials; they serve as Peace Officers; learn and apply Vehicle and Traffic Laws, Penal Law, Criminal Procedure Law, and Triborough Bridge and Tunnel Rules and Regulations; know and enforce rules concerning transportation of hazardous materials, and assist at accidents involving hazardous materials; perform various administrative duties; occasionally supervise other employees; and perform related work.

Some of the physical activities performed by Bridge and Tunnel Officers include lifting and carrying heavy objects, climbing onto structures and vehicles, shoveling snow and removing debris from the roadways; and providing emergency assistance to motorists involved in traffic accidents. They must understand verbal communication and be able to communicate clearly over the radio with background noise, and read and write under low light conditions.

Bridge and Tunnel Officers work outdoors in all kinds of weather; walk and/or stand in an assigned area during a tour; drive or sit in a patrol car; operate emergency vehicles; and may be physically active for prolonged periods of time. Bridge and Tunnel Officers must often deal with highly stressful situations while remaining calm and courteous.

THE TEST: You will be given a multiple-choice test. Your score on this test will determine 100% of your final score and will be used to determine your place on an eligible list. The pass mark will be announced at a later date. The multiple-choice test may include questions which require any of the following abilities:

Written Comprehension –	understanding written sentences and paragraphs.
Written Expression –	using English words and sentences in writing so others will understand.
Memorization –	remembering new information, such as words, numbers, pictures, and procedures. Pieces of information can be remembered by themselves or with other pieces of information.
Problem Sensitivity –	being able to recognize when something is wrong or is likely to go wrong. It includes being able to identify the whole problem as well as the elements of the problem.
Mathematical Reasoning –	being able to understand and organize a problem and then to select a mathematical method or formula to solve it.
Number Facility –	adding, subtracting, multiplying, and dividing numbers quickly and correctly, also as steps in other operations like finding percentages, calculating weighted averages, etc.
Deductive Reasoning –	applying general rules to specific problems or cases to come up with correct solutions or obtain logical answers.
Inductive Reasoning –	combining separate pieces of information, or specific answers to problems, to form general rules or conclusions. It involves the ability to think of possible reasons why things go together or events are connected.
Information Ordering –	following correctly a rule or set of rules in a certain order or proper sequence to put in order things or actions such as numbers, letters, words, sentences, procedures, pictures, and mathematical or logical operations.
Visualization –	imagining how pictures or objects would look if moved around or rearranged.
Spatial Orientation –	being able to tell where you are in relation to the location of some object or to tell where the object is in relation to you.

HOW TO TAKE A TEST

I. YOU MUST PASS AN EXAMINATION

A. WHAT EVERY CANDIDATE SHOULD KNOW

Examination applicants often ask us for help in preparing for the written test. What can I study in advance? What kinds of questions will be asked? How will the test be given? How will the papers be graded?

As an applicant for a civil service examination, you may be wondering about some of these things. Our purpose here is to suggest effective methods of advance study and to describe civil service examinations.

Your chances for success on this examination can be increased if you know how to prepare. Those "pre-examination jitters" can be reduced if you know what to expect. You can even experience an adventure in good citizenship if you know why civil service examinations are given.

B. WHY ARE CIVIL SERVICE EXAMINATIONS GIVEN?

Civil service examinations are important to you in two ways. As a citizen, you want public jobs filled by employees who know how to do their work. As a job-seeker, you want a fair chance to compete for that job on an equal footing with other candidates. The best known means of accomplishing this two-fold goal is the competitive examination.

Examinations are widely publicized throughout the nation. They may be administered for jobs in federal, state, city, municipal, town, or village governments or agencies.

Any citizen may apply, with some limitations, such as the age or residence of applicants. Your experience and education may be reviewed to see whether you meet the requirements for the particular examination. When these requirements exist, they are reasonable and are applied consistently to all applicants. Thus, a competitive examination may cause you some uneasiness now, but it is your privilege and safeguard.

C. HOW ARE CIVIL SERVICE EXAMINATIONS DEVELOPED?

Examinations are carefully written by trained technicians who are specialists in the field known as "psychological measurement," in consultation with recognized authorities in the field of work that the test will cover. These experts recommend the subject matter areas or skills to be tested; only those knowledges or skills important to your success on the job are included. The most reliable books and source materials available are used as references. Together, the experts and technicians judge the difficulty level of the questions.

Test technicians know how to phrase questions so that the problem is clearly stated. Their ethics do not permit "trick" or "catch" questions. Questions may have been tried out on sample groups, or subjected to statistical analysis, to determine their usefulness.

Written tests are often used in combination with performance tests, ratings of training and experience, and oral interviews. All of these measures combine to form the best known means of finding the right man for the right job.

II. HOW TO PASS THE WRITTEN TEST

A. NATURE OF THE EXAMINATION

To prepare intelligently for civil service examinations, you should know how they differ from school examinations you have taken. In school you were assigned certain definite pages to read or subjects to cover. The examination questions were quite detailed and usually emphasized memory. Civil service examinations, on the other hand, try to discover your present ability to perform the duties of a position, plus your potentiality to learn these duties. In other words, a civil service examination attempts to predict how successful you will be. Questions cover such a broad area that they cannot be as minute and detailed as school examination questions.

In the public service similar kinds of work, or positions, are grouped together in one "class." This process is known as "position-classification." All the positions in a class are paid according to the salary range for that class. One class title covers all these positions, and they are all tested by the same examination.

B. FOUR BASIC STEPS

1. Study the Announcement.--How, then, can you know what subjects to study? Our best answer is: "Learn as much as possible about the class of positions for which you have applied." The examination will test the knowledge, skills, and abilities needed to do the work.

Your most valuable source of information about the position you want is the official announcement of the examination. This announcement lists the training and experience qualifications. Check these standards and apply only if you come reasonably close to meeting them.

The brief description of the position in the examination announcement offers some clues to the subjects which will be tested. Think about the job itself. Review the duties in your mind. Can you perform them, or are there some in which you are rusty? Fill in the blank spots in your preparation.

Many jurisdictions preview the written test in the examination announcement by including a section called "Knowledge and Abilities Required," "Scope of Examination," or some similar heading. Here you will find out specifically what fields will be tested.

2. Review Your Own Background.-- Once you learn in general what the position is all about, and what you need to know to do the work, ask yourself which subjects you already know fairly well and which need improvement. You may wonder whether to concentrate on improving your strong areas or on building some background in your fields of weakness. When the announcement has specified "some knowledge" or "considerable knowledge," or has used adjectives such as "beginning principles of ...." or "advanced .....methods," you can get a clue as to the number and difficulty of questions to be asked in any given field. More questions, and hence broader coverage, would be included for those subjects which are more important in the work. Now weigh your strengths and weaknesses against the job requirements and prepare accordingly.

3. Determine the Level of the Position.-- Another way to tell how intensively you should prepare is to understand the level of the job for which you are applying. Is it the entering level? In other words, is this the position in which beginners in a field of work are hired? Or is it an intermediate or advanced level? Sometimes this is indicated by such words as "Junior" or "Senior" in the class title.Other jurisdictions use Roman numerals to designate the level: Clerk I,

Clerk II, for example. The word "Supervisor" sometimes appears in the title. If the level is not indicated by the title, check the description of duties. Will you be working under very close supervision, or will you have responsibility for independent decisions in this work?

4. Choose Appropriate Study Materials. -- Now that you know the subjects to be examined and the relative amount of each subject to be covered, you can choose suitable study materials. For beginning level jobs, or even advanced ones, if you have a pronounced weakness in some aspect of your training, read a modern, standard textbook in that field. Be sure it is up-to-date and has general coverage. Such books are normally available at your library, and the librarian will be glad to help you locate one. For entry level positions, questions of appropriate difficulty are chosen -- neither highly advanced questions, nor those too simple. Such questions require careful thought but not advanced training.

If the position for which you are applying is technical or advanced, you will read more advanced, specialized material. If you are already familiar with the basic principles of your field, elementary textbooks would waste your time. Concentrate on advanced textbooks and technical periodicals. Think through the concepts and review difficult problems in your field.

These are all general sources. You can get more ideas on your own initiative, following these leads. For example, training manuals and publications of the government agency which employs workers in your field can be useful, particularly for technical and professional positions. A letter or visit to the government department involved may result in more specific study suggestions, and certainly will provide you with a more definite idea of the exact nature of the position you are seeking.

III. KINDS OF TESTS

Tests are used for purposes other than measuring knowledge and ability to perform specified duties. For some positions, it is equally important to test ability to make adjustments to new situations or to profit from training. In others, basic mental abilities not dependent upon information are essential. Questions which test these things may not appear as pertinent to the duties of the position as those which test for knowledge and information. Yet they are often highly important parts of a fair examination. For very general questions, it is almost impossible to help you direct your study efforts. What we can do is to point out some of the more common of these general abilities needed in public service positions and describe some typical questions.

1. General Information

Broad, general information has been found useful for predicting job success in some kinds of work. This is tested in a variety of ways, from vocabulary lists to questions about current events. Basic background in some field of work, such as sociology or economics, may be sampled in a group of questions. Often these are principles which have become familiar to most persons through "exposure" rather than through formal training. It is difficult to advise you how to study for these questions; being alert to the world around you is our best suggestion.

2. Verbal Ability

An example of an ability needed in many positions is verbal or language ability. Verbal ability is, in brief, the ability to use and understand words. Vocabulary and grammar tests are typical measures of this ability. "Reading comprehension" or "paragraph interpretation" questions are common in many kinds of civil service tests. You are given a paragraph of written material and asked to find its central meaning.

3. Numerical Ability

Number skills can be tested by the familiar arithmetic problem, by checking paired lists of numbers to see which are alike and which are different, or by interpreting charts and graphs. In the latter test, a graph may be printed in the test booklet which you are asked to use as the basis for answering questions.

4. Observation

A popular test for law-enforcement positions is the observation test. A picture is shown to you for several minutes, then taken away. Questions about the picture test your ability to observe both details and larger elements.

5. Following Directions

In many positions in the public service, the employee must be able to carry out written instructions dependably and accurately. You may be given a chart with several columns, each column listing a variety of information. The questions require you to carry out directions involving the information given in the chart.

6. Skills and Aptitudes

Performance tests effectively measure some manual skills and aptitudes. When the skill is one in which you are trained, such as typing or shorthand, you can practice. These tests are often very much like those given in business school or high school courses. For many of the other skills and aptitudes, however, no short-time preparation can be made. Skills and abilities natural to you or that you have developed throughout your lifetime are being tested.

Many of the general questions just described provide all the data needed to answer the questions and ask you to use your reasoning ability to find the answers. Your best preparation for these tests, as well as for tests of facts and ideas, is to be at your physical and mental best. You, no doubt, have your own methods of getting into an exam-taking mood and keeping "in shape." The next section lists some ideas on this subject.

IV. KINDS OF QUESTIONS

Only rarely is the "essay" question, which you answer in narrative form, used in civil service tests. Civil service tests are usually of the short-answer type. Full instructions for answering these questions will be given to you at the examination. But in case this is your first experience with short-answer questions and separate answer sheets, here is what you need to know.

1. Multiple-Choice Questions

Most popular of the short-answer questions is the "multiple-choice" or "best-answer" question. It can be used, for example, to test for factual knowledge, ability to solve problems, or judgment in meeting situations found at work.

A multiple-choice question is normally one of three types:

(1) It can begin with an incomplete statement followed by several possible endings. You are to find the one ending which *best* completes the statement, although some of the others may not be entirely wrong.

(2) It can also be a complete statement in the form of a question which is answered by choosing one of the statements listed.

(3) It can be in the form of a problem -- again you select the best answer.

Here is an example of a multiple-choice question with a discussion which should give you some clues as to the method for choosing the right answer.

SAMPLE QUESTION:

When an employee has a complaint about his assignment, the action which will *best* help him overcome his difficulty is
(A) to discuss his difficulty with his co-workers
(B) to take the problem to the head of the organization
(C) to take the problem to the person who gave him the assignment
(D) to say nothing to anyone about his complaint

In answering this question you should study each of the choices to find which is best. Consider choice (A). Certainly an employee may discuss his complaint with fellow employees, but no change or improvement can result, and the complaint remains unsolved. Choice (B) is a poor choice since the head of the organization probably does not know what assignment you have been given, and taking your problem to him is known as "going over the head" of the supervisor. The supervisor, or person who made the assignment, is the person who can clarify it or correct any injustice. Choice (C) is, therefore, correct. To say nothing, as in choice (D), is unwise. Supervisors have an interest in knowing the problems employees are facing, and the employee is seeking a solution to his problem.

2. True-False Questions

The "true-false" or "right-wrong" form of question is sometimes used. Here a complete statement is given. Your problem is to decide whether the statement is right or wrong.

SAMPLE QUESTION:

A person-to-person long distance telephone call costs less than a station-to-station call to the same city.

This question is wrong, or "false," since person-to-person calls are more expensive.

This is not a complete list of all possible question forms, although most of the others are variations of these common types. You will always get complete directions for answering questions. Be sure you understand *how* to mark your answers -- ask questions until you do.

V. RECORDING YOUR ANSWERS

For an examination with very few applicants, you may be told to record your answers in the test booklet itself. Separate answer sheets are much more common. If this separate answer sheet is to be scored by machine -- and this is often the case -- it is highly important that you mark your answers correctly in order to get credit.

An electric test-scoring machine is often used in civil service offices because of the speed with which papers can be scored. Machine-scored answer sheets must be marked with a special pencil, which will be given to you. This pencil has a high graphite content which responds to the electrical scoring machine. As a matter of fact, stray dots may register as answers, so do not let your pencil rest on the answer sheet while you are pondering the correct answer. Also, if your pencil lead breaks or is otherwise defective, ask for another.

Since the answer sheet will be dropped in a slot in the scoring machine, be careful not to bend the corners or get the paper crumpled.

The answer sheet normally has five vertical columns of numbers, with 30 numbers to a column. These numbers correspond to the question numbers in your test booklet. After each number, going across the page, are four or five pairs of dotted lines. These short dotted lines have small letters or numbers above them. The first two pairs may also have a "T" and "F" above the letters. This indicates that the first two pairs only are to be used if the questions are of the true-false type. If the questions are multiple-choice, disregard this "T" and "F" completely, and pay attention only to the small number or letters.

Answer your questions in the manner of the sample that follows. Proceed in the sequential steps outlined below.

Assume that you are answering question 32, which is:

32. The largest city in the United States is:
    A. Washington, D.C.   B. New York City   C. Chicago
    D. Detroit   E. San Francisco

1. Choose the answer you think is best.
    New York City is the largest, so choice B is correct.
2. Find the row of dotted lines numbered the same as the question you are answering.
    This is question number 32, so find row number 32.
3. Find the pair of dotted lines corresponding to the answer you have chosen.
    You have chosen answer B, so find the pair of dotted lines marked "B".
4. Make a solid black mark between the dotted lines.
    Go up and down two or three times with your pencil so plenty of graphite rubs off, but do not let the mark get outside or above the dots.

VI. BEFORE THE TEST

Common sense will help you find procedures to follow to get ready for an examination. Too many of us, however, overlook these sensible measures. Indeed, nervousness and fatigue have been found to be the most serious reasons why applicants fail to do their best on civil service tests. Here is a list of reminders.

1. Begin Your Preparation Early

Don't wait until the last minute to go scurrying around for books and materials or to find out what the position is all about.

2. Prepare Continuously

An hour a night for a week is better than an all-night cram session. This has been definitely established. What is more, a night a week for a month will return better dividends than crowding your study into a shorter period of time.

3. Locate the Place of the Examination

You have been sent a notice telling you when and where to report for the examination. If the location is in a different town or otherwise unfamiliar to you, it would be well to inquire the best route and learn something about the building.

4. Relax the Night Before the Test

Allow your mind to rest. Do not study at all that night. Plan some mild recreation or diversion; then go to bed early and get a good night's sleep.

5. Get Up Early Enough to Make a Leisurely Trip to the Place for the Test

Then unforeseen events, traffic snarls, unfamiliar buildings, will not upset you.

6. Dress Comfortably

A written test is not a fashion show. You will be known by number and not by name, so wear something comfortable.

7. Leave Excess Paraphernalia at Home

Shopping bags and odd bundles will get in your way. You need bring only the items mentioned in the official notice sent to you; usually everything you need is provided. Do not bring reference books to the examination. They will only confuse those last minutes and be taken away from you when in the test room.

8. Arrive Somewhat Ahead of Time

If because of transportation schedules you must get there very early, bring a newspaper or magazine to take your mind off yourself while waiting.

9. Locate the Examination Room

When you have found the proper room, you will be directed to the seat or part of the room where you will sit. Sometimes you are given a sheet of instructions to read while you are waiting. Do not fill out any forms until you are told to do so; just read them and be ready.

10. Relax and Prepare to Listen to the Instructions

11. If you have any physical problem that may keep you from doing your best, be sure to tell the test administrator. If you are sick, or in poor health, you really cannot do your best on the test. You can come back and take the test some other time.

VII. AT THE TEST

The day of the test is here and you have the test booklet in your hand. The temptation to get going is very strong. Caution! There is more to success than knowing the right answers. You must know how to identify your papers and understand variations in the type of short-answer question used in this particular examination. Follow these suggestions for maximum results from your efforts:

1. Cooperate with the Monitor

The test administrator has a duty to create a situation in which you can be as much at ease as possible. He will give instructions, tell you when to begin, check to see that you are marking your answer sheet correctly. He is not there to guard you, although he will see that your competitors do not take unfair advantage. He wants to help you do your best.

2. Listen to All Instructions

Don't jump the gun! Wait until you understand all directions. In most civil service tests you get more time than you need to answer the questions. So don't get in a hurry. Read each word of instructions until you clearly understand the meaning. Study the examples. Listen to all announcements. Follow directions. Ask questions if you do not understand what to do.

3. Identify Your Papers

Civil service examinations are usually identified by number only. You will be assigned a number; you must not put your name on your test papers. Be sure to copy your number correctly. Since more than one examination may be given, copy your exact examination title.

4. Plan Your Time

Unless you are told that a test is a "speed" or "rate-of-work" test, speed itself is not usually important. Time enough to answer all the questions will be provided. But this does not mean that you have all day. An overall time limit has been set. Divide the total time (in minutes) by the number of questions to get the approximate time you have for each question.

5. Do Not Linger Over Difficult Questions

If you come across a difficult question, mark it with a paper clip (useful to have along) and come back to it when you have been through the booklet. One caution if you do this -- be sure to skip a number on your answer sheet too. Check often to be sure that you have not lost your place and that you are marking in the row numbered the same as the question you are answering.

6. Read the Questions

Be sure you know what the question asks! Many capable people are unsuccessful because they failed to *read* the questions correctly.

7. Answer All Questions

Unless you have been instructed that a penalty will be deducted for incorrect answers, it is better to guess than to omit a question.

8. Speed Tests

It is often better *not* to guess on speed tests. It has been found that on timed tests people are tempted to spend the last few seconds before time is called in marking answers at random -- without even reading them -- in the hope of picking up a few extra points. To discourage this practice, the instructions may warn you that your score will be "corrected" for guessing. That is, a penalty will be applied. The incorrect answers will be deducted from the correct ones, or some other penalty formula will be used.

9. Review Your Answers

If you finish before time is called, go back to the questions you guessed or omitted to give further thought to them. Review other answers if you have time.

10. Return Your Test Materials

If you are ready to leave before others have finished or time is called, take *all* your materials to the monitor and leave quietly. **Never take any test material with you. The monitor can discover whose papers are not complete, and taking a test booklet may be grounds for disqualification.**

VIII. EXAMINATION TECHNIQUES

1. Read the *general* instructions carefully. These are usually printed on the first page of the examination booklet. As a rule, these instructions refer to the timing of the examination; the fact that you should not start work until the signal and must stop work at a signal, etc. If there are any *special* instructions, such as a choice of questions to be answered, make sure that you note this instruction carefully.

2. When you are ready to start work on the examination, that is as soon as the signal has been given, read the instructions to each question booklet, underline any key words or phrases, such as *least, best, outline, describe,* and the like. In this way you will tend to answer as requested rather than discover on reviewing your paper that you *listed without describing,* that you selected the *worst* choice rather than the *best* choice, etc.

3. If the examination is of the objective or so-called multiple-choice type, that is, each question will also give a series of possible answers: A, B, C, or D, and you are called upon to select the best answer and write the letter next to that answer on your answer paper, it is advisable to start answering each question in turn. There may be anywhere from 50 to 100 such questions in the three or four hours allotted and you can see how much time would be taken if you read through all the questions before beginning to answer any. Furthermore, if you come across a question or a group of questions which you know would be difficult to answer, it would undoubtedly affect your handling of all the other questions.

4. If the examination is of the esssay-type and contains but a few questions, it is a moot point as to whether you should read all the questions before starting to answer any one. Of course if you are given a choice, say five out of seven and the like, then it is essential to read all the questions so you can eliminate the two which are most difficult. If, however, you are asked to answer all the questions, there may be danger in trying to answer the easiest one first because you may find that you will spend too much time on it. The best technique is to answer the first question, then proceed to the second, etc.

5. Time your answers. Before the examination begins, write down the time it started, then add the time allowed for the examination and write down the time it must be completed, then divide the time available somewhat as follows:

(a) If $3\frac{1}{2}$ hours are allowed, that would be 210 minutes. If you have 80 objective-type questions, that would be an average of $2\frac{1}{2}$ minutes per question. Allow yourself no more than 2 minutes per question, or a total of 160 minutes, which will permit about 50 minutes to review.

(b) If for the time allotment of 210 minutes, there are 7 essay questions to answer, that would average about 30 minutes a question. Give yourself only 25 minutes per question so that you have about 35 minutes to review.

6. The most important instruction is *to read each question* and make sure you know what is wanted. The second most important instruction is to *time yourself properly* so that you answer every question. The third most important instruction is to *answer every question*. Guess if you have to but include something for each question. Remember that you will receive no credit for a blank and will probably receive some credit if you write something in answer to an essay question. If you guess a letter, say "B" for a multiple-choice question, you may have guessed right. If you leave a blank as the answer to a multiple-choice question, the examiners may respect your feelings but it will not add a point to your score.

7. Suggestions

   a. <u>Objective-Type Questions</u>

     (1) Examine the question booklet for proper sequence of pages and questions.

     (2) Read all instructions carefully.

     (3) Skip any question which seems too difficult; return to it after all other questions have been answered.

     (4) Apportion your time properly; do not spend too much time on any single question or group of questions.

     (5) Note and underline key words -- *all, most, fewest, least, best, worst, same, opposite.*

     (6) Pay particular attention to negatives.

     (7) Note unusual option, e.g., unduly long, short, complex, different or similar in content to the body of the question.

     (8) Observe the use of "hedging" words -- *probably, may, most likely, etc.*

     (9) Make sure that your answer is put next to the same number as the question.

     (10) Do not second-guess unless you have good reason to believe the second answer is definitely more correct.

     (11) Cross out original answer if you decide another answer is more accurate; do not erase.

     (12) Answer all questions; guess unless instructed otherwise.

     (13) Leave time for review.

   b. <u>Essay-Type Questions</u>

     (1) Read each question carefully.

     (2) Determine exactly what is wanted. Underline key words or phrases.

     (3) Decide on outline or paragraph answer.

     (4) Include many different points and elements unless asked to develop any one or two points or elements.

     (5) Show impartiality by giving pros and cons unless directed to select one side only.

     (6) Make and write down any assumptions you find necessary to answer the question.

     (7) Watch your English, grammar, punctuation, choice of words.

     (8) Time your answers; don't crowd material.

8. Answering the Essay Question

   Most essay questions can be answered by framing the specific response around several key words or ideas. Here are a few such key words or ideas:

M's: manpower, materials, methods, money, management;
P's: purpose, program, policy, plan, procedure, practice, problems, pitfalls, personnel, public relations.

a. <u>Six Basic Steps in Handling Problems</u>:
   (1) **Preliminary** plan and background development
   (2) **Collect** information, data and facts
   (3) **Analyze** and interpret information, data and facts
   (4) **Analyze** and develop solutions as well as make recommendations
   (5) **Prepare** report and sell recommendations
   (6) **Install** recommendations and follow up effectiveness

b. <u>Pitfalls to Avoid</u>
   (1) *Taking things for granted*
       A statement of the situation does not necessarily imply that each of the elements is necessarily true; for example, a complaint may be invalid and biased so that all that can be taken for granted is that a complaint has been registered.
   (2) *Considering only one side of a situation*
       Wherever possible, indicate several alternatives and then point out the reasons you selected the best one.
   (3) *Failing to indicate follow-up*
       Whenever your answer indicates action on your part, make certain that you will take proper follow-up action to see how successful your recommendations, procedures, or actions turn out to be.
   (4) *Taking too long in answering any single question*
       Remember to time your answers properly.

IX. AFTER THE TEST

Scoring procedures differ in detail among civil service jurisdictions although the general principles are the same. Whether the papers are hand-scored or graded by the electric scoring machine we have described, they are nearly always graded by number. That is, the person who marks the paper knows only the number -- never the name -- of the applicant. Not until all the papers have been graded will they be matched with names. If other tests, such as training and experience or oral interview ratings have been given, scores will be combined. Different parts of the examination usually have different weights. For example, the written test might count 60 percent of the final grade, and a rating of training and experience 40 percent. In many jurisdictions, veterans will have a certain number of points added to their grades.

After the final grade has been determined, the names are placed in grade order and an eligible list is established. There are various methods for resolving ties between those who get the same final grade: probably the most common is to place first the name of the person whose application was received first. Job offers are made from the eligible list in the order the names appear on it.

You will be notified of your grade and your rank order as soon as all these computations have been made. This will be done as rapidly as possible.

People who are found to meet the requirements in the announcement are called "eligibles." Their names are put on a list of eligibles. An eligible's chances of getting a job depend on how high he stands on this list and how fast agencies are filling jobs from the list.

When a job is to be filled from a list of eligibles, the agency asks for the names of people on the list of eligibles for that job.

When the civil service commission receives this request, it sends to the agency the names of the three people highest on the list. Or, if the job to be filled has specialized requirements, the office sends the agency, from the general list, the names of the top three persons who meet those requirements.

The appointing officer makes a choice from among the three people whose names were sent to him. If the selected person accepts the appointment, the names of the others are put back on the list to be considered for future openings.

That is the rule in hiring from all kinds of eligible lists, whether they are for typist, carpenter, chemist, or something else. For every vacancy, the appointing officer has his choice of any one of the top three eligibles on the list. This explains why the person whose name is on top of the list sometimes does not get an appointment when some of the persons lower on the list do. If the appointing officer chooses the No.2 or No.3 eligible, the No.1 eligible does not get a job at once, but stays on the list until he is appointed or the list is terminated.

X. HOW TO PASS THE INTERVIEW TEST

The examination for which you applied requires an oral interview test. You have already taken the written test and you are now being called for the interview test -- the final part of the formal examination.

You may think that it is not possible to prepare for an interview test and that there are no procedures to follow during an interview.

Our purpose is to point out some things you can do in advance that will help you and some good rules to follow and pitfalls to avoid while you are being interviewed.

A. *WHAT IS AN INTERVIEW SUPPOSED TO TEST?*

The written examination is designed to test the technical knowledge and competence of the candidate; the oral is designed to evaluate intangible qualities, not readily measured otherwise, and to establish a list showing the relative fitness of each candidate, *as measured against his competitors*, for the position sought. Scoring is not on the basis of "right" or "wrong," but on a sliding scale of values ranging from "not passable" to "outstanding." As a matter of fact, it is possible to achieve a relatively low score without a single "incorrect" answer because of evident weakness in the qualities being measured,

Occasionally, an examination may consist entirely of an oral test -- either an individual or a group oral. In such cases, information is sought concerning the technical knowledges and abilities of the candidate, since there has been no written examination for this purpose. More commonly, however, an oral test is used to supplement a written examination.

B. *WHO CONDUCTS INTERVIEWS?*

The composition of oral boards varies among different jurisdictions. In nearly all, a representative of the personnel department serves as chairman. One of the members of the board may be a representative of the department in which the candidate would work. In some cases, "outside experts" are used, and, frequently, a business man or some other representative of the general public is asked to serve. Labor and management or other special groups may be represented. The aim is to secure the services of experts in the appropriate field.

However the board is composed, it is a good idea (and not at all improper or unethical) to ascertain in advance of the interview who the members are and what groups they represent. When you are introduced to them, you will have some idea of their backgrounds and interests, and at least you will not stutter and stammer over their names.

C. *WHAT TO DO BEFORE THE INTERVIEW*

While knowledge about the board members is useful and takes some of the surprise element out of the interview, there is other preparation which is more substantive. It *is* possible to prepare for an oral -- in several ways:

1. Keep a Copy of Your Application and Review it Carefully Before the Interview

   This may be the only document before the oral board, and the starting point of the interview. Know what experience and education you have listed there, and the sequence and dates of it. Sometimes the board will ask *you* to review the highlights of your experience for them; you should not have to hem and haw doing it.

2. Study the Class Specification and the Examination Announcement

   Usually, the oral board has one or both of these to guide them. The qualities, characteristics, or knowledges required by the position sought are stated in these documents. They offer valuable clues as to the nature of the oral interview. For example, if the job involves supervisory responsibilities, the announcement will usually indicate that knowledge of modern supervisory methods and the qualifications of the candidate as a supervisor will be tested. If so, you can expect such questions, frequently in the form of a hypothetical situation which you are expected to solve. *Never* go into an oral without knowledge of the duties and responsibilities of the job you seek.

3. Think Through Each Qualification Required

   Try to visualize the kind of questions *you* would ask if you were a board member. How well could you answer them? Try especially to appraise your own knowledge and background in each area, *measured against the job sought,* and identify any areas in which you are weak. Be critical and realistic -- do not flatter yourself.

4. Do Some General Reading in Areas in Which You Feel You May be Weak

   For example, if the job involves supervision and your past experience has *not,* some general reading in supervisory methods and practices, particularly in the field of human relations, might be useful. *Do not* study agency procedures or detailed manuals. The oral board will be testing your understanding and capacity, *not* your memory.

5. Get a Good Night's Sleep and Watch Your General Health and Mental Attitude

   You will want a clear head at the interview. Take care of a cold or other minor ailment, and, of course, *no hangovers*.

D. WHAT TO DO THE DAY OF THE INTERVIEW

Now comes the day of the interview itself. Give yourself plenty of time to get there. Plan to arrive somewhat ahead of the scheduled time, particularly if your appointment is in the fore part of the day. If a previous candidate fails to appear, the board might be ready for you a bit early. By early afternoon an oral board is almost invariably behind schedule if there are many candidates, and you may have to wait. Take along a book or magazine to read, or your application to review. But leave any extraneous material in the waiting room when you go in for your interview. In any event, relax and compose yourself.

The matter of dress is important. The board is forming impressions about you -- from your experience, your manners, your attitudes, and from your appearance. Give your personal appearance careful attention. Dress your *best*, but not your flashiest. Choose conservative, appropriate clothing, and be sure it and you are immaculate. This is a business interview, and your appearance should indicate that you regard it as such. Besides, being well-groomed and properly dressed will help boost your confidence.

Sooner or later, someone will call your name and escort you into the interview room. *This is it.* From here on you are on your own. It is too late for any more preparation. But, remember, you asked for this opportunity to prove your fitness, and you are here because your request was granted.

E. WHAT HAPPENS WHEN YOU GO IN?

The usual sequence of events will be as follows: The clerk (who is often the board stenographer) will introduce you to the chairman of the oral board, who will introduce you to each other member of the board. Acknowledge the introductions before you sit down. Do not be surprised if you find a microphone facing you or a stenotypist sitting by. Oral interviews are usually recorded, in the event of an appeal or other review.

Usually the chairman of the board will open the interview by reviewing the highlights of your education and work experience from your application -- primarily for the benefit of the other members of the board, as well as to get the material into the record. Do not interrupt or comment unless there is an error or significant misinterpretation; if so, do not hesitate. But do not quibble about insignificant matters. Usually, also, he will ask you some question about your education, your experience, or your present job -- partly to get you started talking, to establish the interviewing "rapport." He may start the actual questioning, or turn it over to one of the other members. Frequently each member undertakes the questioning on a particular area, one in which he is perhaps most competent. So you can expect each member to participate in the examination. And because the time is limited, you may expect some rather abrupt switches in the direction the questioning takes. Do not be upset by it. Normally, a board member will not pursue a single line of questioning unless he discovers a particular strength or weakness.

After each member has participated, the chairman will usually ask whether any member has any further questions, then will ask you if you have anything you wish to add. Unless you are expecting this question, it may floor you. Or worse, it may start you off on an extended, extemporaneous speech. The board is not usually seeking more information. The question is principally to offer you a last opportunity to present further qualifications or to indicate that you have nothing to add. So, if you feel that a significant qualification or characteristic has been overlooked, it is proper to point it out in a sentence or so. Do not compliment the board on the thoroughness of their examination -- they have been sketchy, and you know it. If you wish, merely say, "No thank you, I have nothing further to add." This is a point where you can "talk yourself out" of a good impression or fail to present an important bit of information. *Remember, you close the interview yourself.*

The chairman will then say,"That is all,Mr.Smith,thank you." Do not be startled; the interview is over, and quicker than you think. Say,"Thank you and good morning," gather up your belongings and take your leave. Save your sigh of relief for the other side of the door.

F. *HOW TO PUT YOUR BEST FOOT FORWARD*

Throughout all this process, you may feel that the board individually and collectively is trying to pierce your defenses, to seek out your hidden weaknesses, and to embarrass and confuse you. Actually, this is not true. They are obliged to make an appraisal of your qualifications for the job you are seeking, and they *want to see you in your best light.* Remember, they must interview all candidates and a noncooperative candidate may become a failure in spite of their best efforts to bring out his qualifications. Here are fifteen(15) suggestions that will help you:

1. Be Natural. Keep Your Attitude Confident,But Not Cocky

If *you* are not confident that you can do the job, do not ex-expect the *board* to be. Do not apologize for your weaknesses, try to bring out your strong points. The board is interested in a positive, not a negative presentation. Cockiness will antagonize any board member, and make him wonder if you are covering up a weakness by a false show of strength.

2. Get Comfortable, But Don't Lounge or Sprawl

Sit erectly but not stiffly. A careless posture may lead the board to conclude you are careless in other things, or at least that you are not impressed by the importance of the occasion to you.Either conclusion is natural, even if incorrect. Do not fuss with your clothing, or with a pencil or an ashtray. Your hands may occasionally be useful to emphasize a point; do not let them become a point of distraction.

3. Do Not Wisecrack or Make Small Talk

This is a serious situation, and your attitude should show that you consider it as such. Further, the time of the board is limited; they do not want to waste it, and neither should you.

4. Do Not Exaggerate Your Experience or Abilities

In the first place, from information in the application,from other interviews and other sources, the board may know more about you than you think; in the second place, you probably will not get away with it in the first place. An experienced board is rather adept at spotting such a situation. Do not take the chance.

5. If You Know a Member of the Board, Do Not Make a Point of It,
   Yet Do Not Hide It.

Certainly you are not fooling him, and probably not the other members of the board. Do not try to take advantage of your acquaintanceship -- it will probably do you little good.

6. Do Not Dominate the Interview

Let the board do that. They will give you the clues -- do not assume that you have to do all the talking. Realize that the board has a number of questions to ask you, and do not try to take up all the interview time by showing off your extensive knowledge of the answer to the first one.

15

7. Be Attentive

You only have twenty minutes or so, and you should keep your attention at its sharpest throughout. When a member is addressing a problem or a question to you, give him your undivided attention. Address your reply principally to him, but do not exclude the other members of the board.

8. Do Not Interrupt

A board member may be stating a problem for you to analyze. He will ask you a question when the time comes. Let him state the problem, and wait for the question.

9. Make Sure You Understand the Question

Do not try to answer until you are sure what the question is. If it is not clear, restate it in your own words or ask the board member to clarify it for you. But do not haggle about minor elements.

10. Reply Promptly But Not Hastily

A common entry on oral board rating sheets is "candidate responded readily," or "candidate hesitated in replies." Respond as promptly and quickly as you can, but do not jump to a hasty, ill-considered answer.

11. Do Not Be Peremptory in Your Answers

A brief answer is proper -- but do not fire your answer back. That is a losing game from your point of view. The board member can probably ask questions much faster than you can answer them.

12. Do Not Try To Create the Answer You Think the Board Member Wants

He is interested in what kind of · mind you have and how it works -- not in playing games. Furthermore, he can usually spot this practice and will usually grade you down on it.

13. Do Not Switch Sides in Your Reply Merely to Agree With a Board Member

Frequently, a member will take a contrary position merely to draw you out and to see if you are willing and able to defend your point of view. Do not start a debate, yet do not surrender a good position. If a position is worth taking, it is worth defending.

] Do Not Be Afraid to Admit an Error in Judgment if You Are Shown to Be Wrong

The board knows that you are forced to reply without any opportunity for careful consideration. Your answer may be demonstrably wrong. If so, admit it and get on with the interview.

15. Do Not Dwell at Length on Your Present Job

The opening question may relate to your present assignment. Answer the question but do not go into an extended discussion. You are being examined for a *new* job, not your present one. As a matter of fact, try to phrase *all* your answers in terms of the job for which you are being examined.

G. BASIS OF RATING

Probably you will forget most of these "do's" and "don'ts" when you walk into the oral interview room. Even remembering them all will not insure you a passing grade. Perhaps you did not have the qualifications in the first place. But remembering them *will* help you to put your best foot forward, without treading on the toes of the board members.

Rumor and popular opinion to the contrary notwithstanding, an oral board wants you to make the best appearance possible. They know you are under pressure -- but they also want to see how you respond to it as a guide to what your reaction would be under the pressures of the job you seek. They will be influenced by the degree of poise you display, the personal traits you show, and the manner in which you respond.

EXAMINATION SECTION

EXAMINATION SECTION

TEST 1

<u>MEMORY BOOKLET</u>

DIRECTIONS: Questions 1 through 6 are based on Memory Scene 1.
Questions 7 through 11 are based on Memory Scene 2.
Study Scene 1 before answering Questions 1 through 6.
Do not refer back while answering. Study Scene 2
before answering Questions 7 through 11. Try to
remember as many details in each scene as you can.
You should pay equal attention both to objects and to
people shown in each scene.

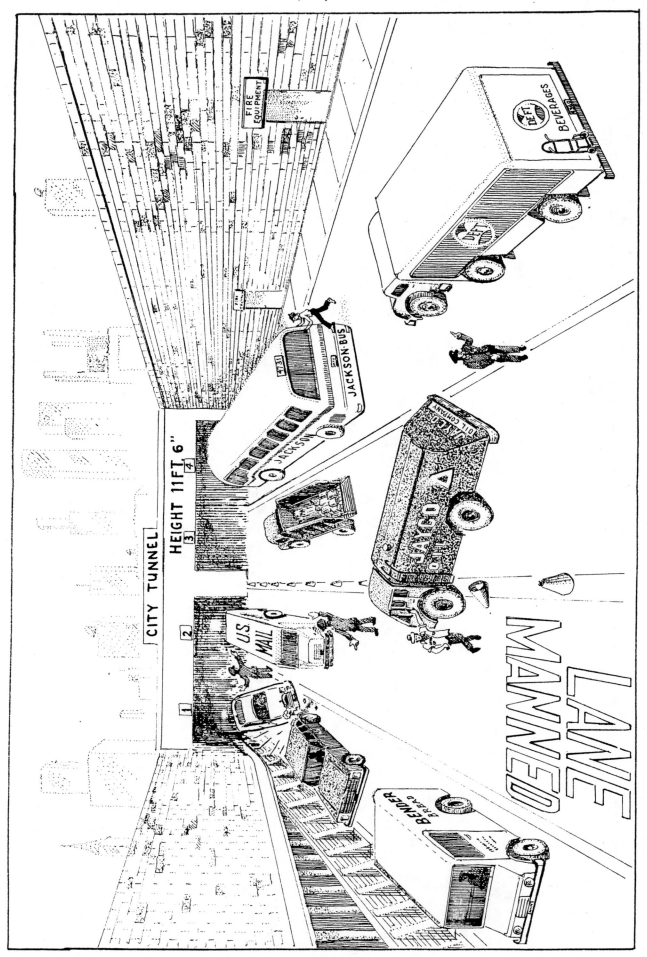

SCENE 1

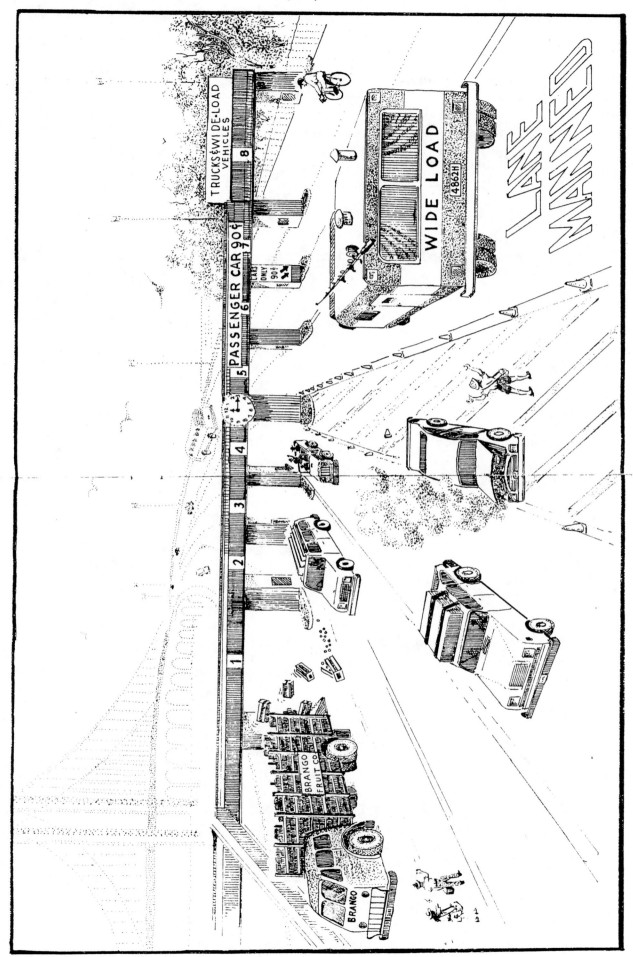

SCENE 2

DIRECTIONS: Each question or incomplete statement is followed by several suggested answers or completions. Select the one that BEST answers the question or completes the statement. *PRINT THE LETTER OF THE CORRECT ANSWER IN THE SPACE AT THE RIGHT.*

Questions 1-6.

DIRECTIONS: Questions 1 through 6 are to be answered on the basis of memory scene 1. Study Scene 1 before answering these questions. Do not refer back while answering. Try to remember as many details in the scene as you can. You should pay equal attention both to objects and to people shown in the scene.

1. The two-car accident is in lane   1.___
    A. 1   B. 2   C. 3   D. 4

2. Which one of the following is printed on the bus?   2.___
    _____ Bus.
    A. Jayco   B. Jackson   C. Jason   D. Bender

3. In the accident, the damage to the fender on the white   3.___
    car is on the _____ side.
    A. *front* passenger's   B. *front* driver's
    C. *rear* passenger's   D. *rear* driver's

4. Which one of the following is printed on the side of the   4.___
    truck that has crossed the center cone line?
    A. Deft Beverages   B. Jackson Oil
    C. Bender Bread   D. Jayco Oil

5. Which one of the following vehicles is being directed by   5.___
    the Bridge and Tunnel Officer in Lane 2?
    A. U.S. Mail truck   B. Bender Bread truck
    C. Mayor Oil Truck   D. Mann Bus

6. The man holding onto the bus is wearing _____ pants and   6.___
    a _____ top.
    A. dark; dark   B. white; dark
    C. dark; white   D. white; white

Questions 7-11.

DIRECTIONS: Questions 7 through 11 are to be answered on the basis of memory scene 2. Study Scene 2 before answering these questions. Do not refer back while answering. Try to remember as many details in the scene as you can. You should pay equal attention both to objects and to people shown in the scene.

7. How many people are standing in Lane 2?   7.___
    A. 2   B. 3   C. 4   D. 5

8. The man on the bicycle is riding toward Toll Lane   8.___
   A. 4   B. 5   C. 8   D. 10

9. The name printed on the vehicle that has boxes falling   9.___
   off the back is _____ Fruit Co.
   A. Branson   B. Brango   C. Mansfield   D. Person's

10. The BEST description of the vehicle in the center striped   10.___
    lane is a
       A. car with boxes tied to the roof
       B. car with the hood raised
       C. car with a flat tire
       D. camper with a fishing pole on its roof

11. Which lane should wide-load vehicles use?   11.___
    A. 6   B. 7   C. 8   D. 9

Questions 12-14.

DIRECTIONS: Questions 12 through 14 are to be answered SOLELY on
               the basis of the following information.

      At 9:20 P.M., Bridge and Tunnel Officers Adams, Bennet, and
Clark respond to a reported accident at the Long Bridge. At the
accident scene, they observe three badly damaged vehicles blocking
the left and center lanes. Only the right lane of the northbound
side is clear for traffic to proceed. The officers begin to clear
the wreckage from the roadway. BTO Bennet receives a call on his
radio to report to the toll plaza, and he departs. Ten minutes
later, at 9:40 P.M., BTO Clark observes a heated argument between
two motorists who are stuck in traffic about 200 feet from the
accident, and he responds to the incident. BTO Davis arrives at
the accident scene to assist in the cleaning of the wreckage. They
complete the assignment and reopen the closed lanes.

12. How many BTOs were at the accident scene when the traffic   12.___
    lanes were reopened?
       A. 1   B. 2   C. 3   D. 4

13. How many lanes does the northbound side of the bridge   13.___
    have?
       A. 1   B. 2   C. 3   D. 4

14. At what time did BTO Bennet leave the accident scene?   14.___
    _____ P.M.
       A. 9:20   B. 9:30   C. 9:40   D. 9:50

15. BTO Jones arrests the driver of a vehicle for driving   15.___
    while intoxicated and escorts him to the local police
    precinct. At the precinct, BTO Jones fills out a voucher
    for all the valuables and cash found in the driver's
    possession.
    The following is a list of these items:
          - 4 twenty-dollar bills
          - 7 ten-dollar bills
          - 8 five-dollar bills
          - 3 silver pens (with receipt) valued at $80.00 each
          - 1 cocktail ring (with receipt) valued at $425.00

What is the TOTAL value of the driver's property?
A. $695   B. $775   C. $805   D. $855

16. Bridge and Tunnel Officer Keller is required to testify   16._
     in court regarding an arrest she made on November 20,
     1987. She reviews the following facts which she recorded
     after making the arrest:

            Arrested Person: Evelyn Edwards
            Charge: Driving While Intoxicated
            Vehicle: 1984 Plymouth Horizon
            Place of Occurrence: Terry River Bridge
            Time of Arrest: 4:20 P.M.

     BTO Keller needs to be accurate and clear when testifying.
     Which one of the following expresses the above information
     MOST clearly and accurately?
     A. On November 20, 1987, I arrested Evelyn Edwards while
        intoxicated at 4:20 P.M. She was driving a 1984
        Plymouth Horizon on the Terry River Bridge.
     B. On November 20, 1987, at 4:20 P.M., Evelyn Edwards
        was driving while intoxicated a 1984 Plymouth Horizon.
        She was arrested on the Terry River Bridge.
     C. Evelyn Edwards was arrested for driving while intoxica-
        ted on the Terry River Bridge at 4:20 P.M. She was
        driving a 1984 Plymouth on November 20, 1987.
     D. Evelyn Edwards was arrested on November 20, 1987 at
        4:20 P.M. on the Terry River Bridge for driving while
        intoxicated. She was driving a 1984 Plymouth Horizon.

17. Bridge and Tunnel Officers who are responsible for collect- 17.
     ing tolls should do the following in the order given:
     A. State the toll amount to the driver.
     B. Call out the amount of money given by the driver.
     C. Press the proper classification button to register
        the toll.
     D. Give change, if any.

18. *Bridge and Tunnel Officers must sometimes rely on eye-*   18._
     witness accounts of incidents, even though eyewitnesses
     may make mistakes with regard to some details.
     Four witnesses tell Officer Farrell that they observed
     a vehicle drive through the plaza without stopping to pay
     the required toll. Following are the descriptions provided
     by the four witnesses.
     Which one of these descriptions should Officer Farrell
     consider MOST likely to be correct?
     A
     A. blue Ford with a dented right fender
     B. gray Ford with a dented right fender
     C. blue Ford with a dented left fender
     D. blue Oldsmobile with a dented right fender

19. A convoy of vehicles approaches BTO Charles in Lane 5 of   19.____
    the toll plaza. The driver of the first car tells BTO
    Charles that he would like to pay for his car and the
    next 19 vehicles which make up his scout troop. The
    following is the list of vehicles in the convoy:

Vehicle Description	Number of Vehicles	Toll Per Vehicle
Passenger car	7	$2.00
Passenger with a one-axle trailer	5	$2.50
Van	3	$3.00
Van with a two-axle trailer	1	$4.00
Passenger Car with a two-axle trailer	4	$3.00

Which one of the following formulas should BTO Charles
use in order to calculate the convoy's TOTAL toll?
    A. (7 × $2.00) + (5 × $2.00) + (4 × $3.00) + (4 × $2.00)
    B. (7 × $2.00) + (5 × $2.50) + (3 × $3.00) + (1 × $4.00)
       + (4 × $3.00)
    C. (12 × $2.00) + (4 × $3.00) + (4 × $3.00)
    D. (12 × $2.00) + (3 × $3.00) + (1 × $4.00) + (4 × $3.00)

20. *Bridge and Tunnel Officers cannot accept counterfeit,*   20.____
    altered, or foreign money for payment of a toll.
    Which one of the following bills should a BTO refuse to
    accept for payment of a toll?
    A(n)
    A. old $20 bill with a serial number that is one digit
       different from a known counterfeit bill
    B. new $50 bill
    C. old $10 bill that has George Washington's face on it
    D. new $10 bill folded in half

Questions 21-23.

DIRECTIONS: Questions 21 through 23 are to be answered SOLELY on
             the basis of the following passage.

Bridge and Tunnel Officers Baker and Clark have been assigned
to cover the toll plaza posts during their 7:00 A.M. to 3:00 P.M.
work tour. After they attended roll call, the BTOs manned their
positions. A motorist pulled into an automatic toll lane, called
to BTO Baker and stated that he had seen a car abandoned in the
middle of the bridge. Mr. John Phillips, the motorist, also stated
that the car was in the right lane with its driver's door open.
He added that a woman with a small child in her arms was walking
on the bridge. BTO Baker informed BTO Clark of the abandoned car
and proceeded to notify Sergeant O'Hara.

BTO Clark was waiting on the toll plaza for a Sergeant to help
him collect the coins from the automatic toll collection machine.
A woman drove to the express toll lane next to where BTO Clark was
standing and asked for assistance. There was a small child with

the woman, and they fit the description of the woman and child seen
on the bridge. BTO Clark notified BTO Baker that there might not
be a need for anyone to investigate the abandoned car since the
driver might have already come down from the bridge. Sergeant
O'Hara was on the toll plaza and had already notified Lieutenant
Fox, stationed in the building, of the problem on the bridge.
The Lieutenant proceeded to drive his patrol car to the middle of
the bridge to investigate.

21. What type of lane did Mr. John Phillips pull into?   21.___
    A(n) _____ lane.
       A. manned   B. closed
       C. automatic toll   D. express

22. Which BTO spoke with the man who drove to the toll plaza?   22.___
       A. Clark   B. O'Hara   C. Fox   D. Baker

23. Who believed that the woman at the toll plaza was the same 23.___
    woman seen walking on the bridge?
       A. O'Hara   B. Fox   C. Clark   D. Baker

24. Bridge and Tunnel Officers will occasionally request   24.___
    additional coins or tokens from a supervisor or Desk
    Officer when their supply runs low.
    Which one of the following would constitute the MOST
    urgent situation for resupply of coins?
    A BTO runs out of dimes
       A. two hours before his lunch period
       B. five minutes before his lunch period
       C. fifteen minutes before the end of his tour
       D. ten minutes before he ends his assignment

25. The following information relates to an incident which   25.___
    occurred while Bridge and Tunnel Officer Henderson was on
    duty:

          Date of Occurrence: January 16, 1988
          Time of Occurrence: 9:15 A.M.
          Place of Occurrence: Toll Lane #39
          Car: Red 1986 Sentra
          Violation: Failure to pay $4.00 toll

    BTO Henderson is preparing a report on the incident.
    Which one of the following expresses the above information
    MOST clearly and accurately?
       A. The driver of a red 1986 Sentra drove through Toll
          Lane #39 on January 16, 1988, at 9:15 A.M., without
          paying the $4.00 toll.
       B. A $4.00 toll was not paid by a motorist. At 9:15
          A.M., a red 1986 Sentra drove through Toll Lane #39
          on January 16, 1988.
       C. A $4.00 toll on January 16, 1988 was not paid. A
          red 1986 Sentra drove through Toll Lane #39 at
          9:15 A.M.
       D. A motorist drove through at 9:15 A.M. on January 16,
          1988. A red 1986 Sentra was in Toll Lane #39 when
          it did not pay the $4.00 toll.

KEY (CORRECT ANSWERS)

1. A		11. C	
2. B		12. B	
3. A		13. C	
4. D		14. B	
5. A		15. D	
6. C		16. D	
7. A		17. C	
8. C		18. A	
9. B		19. B	
10. B		20. C	

21. C
22. D
23. C
24. A
25. A

TEST 2

DIRECTIONS: Each question or incomplete statement is followed by several suggested answers or completions. Select the one that BEST answers the question or completes the statement. *PRINT THE LETTER OF THE CORRECT ANSWER IN THE SPACE AT THE RIGHT.*

1. Bridge and Tunnel Officer Smith responds to an auto fire and obtains the following information at the scene:

   Time of Occurrence: 8:43 P.M.
   License Number: 647-BAG
   Location of Fire on Vehicle: Engine Compartment
   Location of Vehicle: Vine Road, two hundred
                                feet from Mason Street Exit
   Equipment Used: Four fire extinguishers
   Officers Who Responded: Officers Smith and Weston

   BTO Smith is completing a report on the fire.
   Which one of the following expresses the above information MOST clearly and accurately?

   A. At 8:43 P.M., BTOs Smith and Weston responded to a fire two hundred feet from the Mason Street exit on Vine Road on a vehicle, license plate number 647-BAG, in the engine compartment with four fire extinguishers.
   B. At 8:43 P.M., BTOs Smith and Weston used four fire extinguishers on a fire in a vehicle's engine compartment, license plate number 647-BAG. The fire occurred on Vine Road, two hundred feet from the Mason Street exit.
   C. BTOs Smith and Weston were two hundred feet from the Mason Street exit on Vine Road when they responded to a fire using four fire extinguishers on a vehicle's engine compartment, license plate number 647-BAG, at 8:43 P.M.
   D. Two hundred feet from the Mason Street exit on Vine Road, an engine compartment on a vehicle with a license plate number 647-BAG required four fire extinguishers by BTOs Smith and Weston at 8:43 P.M.

Questions 2-3.

DIRECTIONS: Questions 2 and 3 are to be answered SOLELY on the basis of the following information.

   A Bridge and Tunnel Officer issues change to motorists for bills up to and including $100 bills. The BTO must follow the rules listed below when giving change:
   - Always use the smallest number of bills
   - Do not use more than 9 single dollar bills
   - Do not use more than $1 in coins
   - Do not use pennies

- Do not use tokens
- Do not use counterfeit money
- Do not use foreign money

2. What is the MOST appropriate change to be given for a toll of $1.75 when a twenty dollar bill is given by the motorist?

    A. One $10 bill, one $5 bill, three $1 bills, and one quarter
    B. Eighteen $1 bills and one quarter
    C. One $10 bill, eight $1 bills, and one quarter
    D. Three $5 bills, three $1 bills, and one quarter

2.___

3. What is the MOST appropriate change to be given for a $2.25 toll when a $10 bill is given by the motorist?

    A. Seven $1 bills and three quarters
    B. One $5 bill, two $1 bills, and three quarters
    C. One $5 bill, two $1 bills, seven dimes, and five pennies
    D. One $5 bill, one $1 bill, and seven quarters

3.___

4. Bridge and Tunnel Officer Wells responded to a traffic accident and obtained the following information at the scene of the accident:

Date of Occurrence:	January 10, 1988
Place of Occurrence:	Signal Control Station 10, South Tunnel
Time of Occurrence:	7:45 A.M.
Drivers:	Ms. Denise Webb and Mrs. Carol Jones
Action Taken:	Ms. Webb's car was towed from scene

4.___

BTO Wells is reporting the accident to the sergeant. Which one of the following expresses the above information MOST clearly and accurately?

    A. Ms. Denise Webb's car was towed after an accident at 7:45 A.M. from the scene in the South Tunnel at Signal Control Station 10. She was involved with Mrs. Carol Jones in an accident.
    B. Mrs. Carol Jones was in an accident at Signal Control Station 10 in the South Tunnel with Ms. Denise Webb. Her vehicle was towed out of the tunnel at 7:45 A.M.
    C. Ms. Denise Webb and Mrs. Carol Jones were involved in a vehicle accident in the South Tunnel at Signal Control Station 10. Ms. Webb's car was towed from the accident scene at 7:45 A.M.
    D. Ms. Denise Webb's vehicle was towed from the South Tunnel, Signal Control Station 10, after she had an accident with Mrs. Carol Jones at 7:45 A.M.

Questions 5-6.

DIRECTIONS: Questions 5 and 6 are to be answered SOLELY on the basis of the following information.

While working a post at the Franklin Bridge, Bridge and Tunnel Officer Smith is approached by Jane Deere, a motorist on her way home from work. Jane Deere states that there is a teenager running around on the bridge about 100 yards from the facility building. BTO Jones overhears the conversation between Jane Deere and BTO Smith and informs Sgt. Tang of the situation. BTO Smith and Sgt. Tang proceed to investigate the situation. Lt. Jackson, who is in the office, is advised and responds to the scene in a patrol car.

When Lt. Jackson arrives at the scene, BTO Smith and Sgt. Tang are with the teenager and are escorting her toward Lt. Jackson's patrol car. The Sergeant states that the teenager is incoherent and does not know where she is. Lt. Jackson tells the BTO and Sergeant to escort the teenager to the facility building for further questioning.

5.   Who informed Sgt. Tang about the teenager on the bridge?   5.___
     A. BTO Smith   B. Lt. Jackson
     C. Jane Deere   D. BTO Jones

6.   Which two were the FIRST to arrive at the scene of the   6.___
     problem?
         A. Jackson and Jones   B. Deere and Smith
         C. Tang and Smith   D. Jackson and Tang

7.   *Bridge and Tunnel Officers sometimes rely on eyewitness*   7.___
     accounts of incidents, even though eyewitnesses may make
     mistakes with regard to some details.
     Bridge and Tunnel Officer Golden responds to a report of a
     hit and run traffic accident on the bridge. When he arrives,
     he interviews four witnesses who saw the accident occur
     and saw the vehicle leave the scene. The following are
     license plate numbers provided by the four witnesses.
     Which one of these numbers should BTO Golden consider MOST
     likely to be correct?
         A. JK1-799   B. JL2-799   C. JK1-789   D. LK1-696

8.   Bridge and Tunnel Officer Clark is at the scene of a   8.___
     multiple vehicle accident and observes the following:

         Place of Occurrence: Mid span of the William
                                       Street Bridge
         Direction: Southbound
         Vehicles Involved: Two cars and two trucks
         Debris on road: Oil, gas, and glass
         Number of tow trucks needed: Two
         Number of Injured People: Six

     BTO Clark must transmit a description of the accident over
     the radio to the Desk Officer.

Which one of the following expresses the above information MOST clearly and accurately?

   A. On the southbound side at mid span of the William Street Bridge, four vehicles, two cars and two trucks, were involved in an accident with six people injured on the road with oil, gas, and glass. Two tow trucks are needed.

   B. Two cars and two trucks were in an accident at the mid span of the William Street Bridge with oil, gas, and glass on the roadway. Two tow trucks are needed, and there are six injured people on the southbound side.

   C. Six people were injured in a two-truck, two-car accident on the southbound side at mid span of the William Street Bridge. Oil, gas, and glass are on the roadway, and two tow trucks are needed.

   D. Oil, gas, and glass are on the roadway with six injured people and four vehicles, two trucks and two cars. Two tow trucks are needed on the southbound side at mid span of the William Street Bridge.

9. Bridge and Tunnel Officer Fernandez is collecting tolls at the Williams Bridge. A convoy of 14 trucks from the King Trucking Company lines up at his toll lane. The driver of the first truck states that the last driver will pay for all of the trucks. As the trucks pass, BTO Fernandez counts six Class 8 trucks and eight Class 6 trucks. The last driver hands BTO Fernandez a $100 bill. In order for BTO Fernandez to determine the amount of change to be returned, he should

9.____

   A. add eight Class 6 vehicles and six Class 8 vehicles, then multiply the total by $3.75 plus $4.25, then subtract from $100.00

   B. multiply eight Class 6 vehicles by $3.75, then multiply six Class 8 vehicles by $4.25, then add the two amounts together, then subtract from $100.00

   C. multiply six Class 6 vehicles by $3.75, then multiply eight Class 8 vehicles by $4.25, then add the amounts together, then subtract from $100.00

   D. add $3.75 and $4.25, then add eight Class 6 and six Class 8 vehicles, then multiply the totals, then subtract from $100.00

Questions 10-11.

DIRECTIONS: Questions 10 and 11 are to be answered SOLELY on the basis of the following chart.

HENDERSON BRIDGE WEEKEND TOLL COLLECTION INFORMATION FOR MAY

Date	Day	Toll Lane	Average Vehicles Per Hour	Rolls of Tokens Sold	Number of Vehicle Failing to Pay The Toll
May 1	Friday	2	250	15	3
May 2	Saturday	4	175	10	3
May 3	Sunday	6	150	35	5
May 4	Monday	2	225	35	2
May 8	Friday	6	200	25	5
May 9	Saturday	4	100	30	3
May 10	Sunday	8	150	15	0
May 11	Monday	2	225	40	2
May 15	Friday	4	250	25	0
May 16	Saturday	6	100	15	4
May 17	Sunday	8	150	20	2
May 18	Monday	8	100	30	3

10. On which one of the following days should a Bridge and Tunnel Officer at the Henderson Bridge expect to sell AT LEAST 30 rolls of tokens?
     A. Monday   B. Friday   C. Saturday   D. Sunday

11. In which one of the following toll lanes should a Bridge and Tunnel Officer expect to have the GREATEST number of motorists who fail to pay the toll?
     A. 2   B. 4   C. 6   D. 8

12. During the course of BTO Hurst's tour, he received three issues of tokens. The first issue consisted of 35 rolls, the second of 20 rolls, and the third of 15 rolls. At the end of his tour, BTO Hurst returned 7 rolls of tokens to the Desk Officer.
     How many rolls of tokens did he sell during his tour?
     A. 57   B. 62   C. 63   D. 68

13. When assigned to a plaza post at the Gates Bridge, a Bridge and Tunnel Officer's duty is to stop vehicles higher than 12'9".
     Which one of the following situations would an officer be MOST concerned with?
     A
     A. station wagon with two 2 foot square boxes tied to the roof
     B. pick-up truck with ten 12 foot long boards hanging over its tailgate with a red flag tied to them
     C. bus with its sun roof open
     D. 12-foot high truck with cargo 2 feet above the sides

10.___

11.___

12.___

13.___

Questions 14-16.

DIRECTIONS: Questions 14 through 16 are to be answered SOLELY on the basis of the following map. The flow of traffic is indicated by the arrows. If there is only one arrow shown, then traffic flows only in the direction indicated by the arrow. If there are two arrows, then traffic flows in both directions. You must follow the flow of traffic.

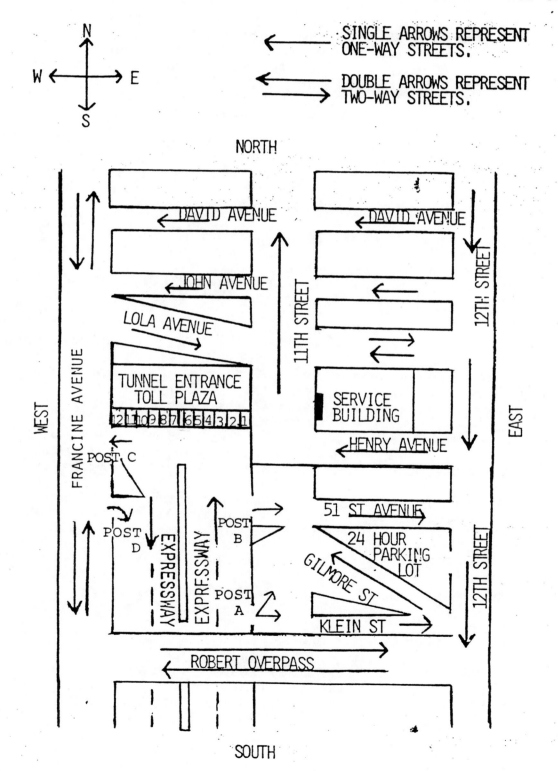

14. Bridge and Tunnel Officer Holland is approached by a   14.___
     motorist at the entrance to the service building. The
     driver asks what is the shortest route to reach the
     southbound expressway.
     Which one of the following is the SHORTEST route for the
     motorist to take making sure to obey all traffic regula-
     tions?
     Travel _____ to enter the expressway.
          A. north on 11th Street to John Avenue, then left on
             John Avenue to Francine Avenue, then left on Francine
             Avenue to Post D, then left at Post D
          B. north on 11th Street to David Avenue, then left on
             David Avenue to Francine Avenue, then left on Francine
             Avenue to Post D, then left at Post D
          C. north on 11th Street to Lola Avenue, then left on
             Lola Avenue to Francine Avenue, then south on Francine
             Avenue to Post D, then left at Post D
          D. south on 11th Street to Henry Avenue, then left on
             Henry Avenue to 12th Street, then right on 12th Street
             to the Robert Overpass, then right on the overpass to
             Francine Avenue, then a right on Francine Avenue to
             Post D, then a right at Post D

15. While exiting the Toll Plaza at Post C, a motorist stops   15.___
     his vehicle and asks BTO Vance, stationed at Post C, for
     directions to the 24 Hour Parking Lot.
     Which one of the following is the SHORTEST route for the
     motorist to take making sure to obey all traffic regula-
     tions?
     Travel _____ into the parking lot.
          A. south on Francine Avenue, then east on Robert Overpass,
             then north on 12th Street, then left
          B. north on Francine Avenue, then southeast on Lola
             Avenue, then south on 12th Street, then right
          C. south on Francine Avenue, then east on Robert Overpass,
             then north on 12th Street, then right
          D. north on Francine Avenue, then southeast on Lola
             Avenue, then south on 11th Street, then east on Henry
             Avenue, then south on 12th Street, then right

16. A motorist is heading north on the expressway toward the   16.___
     toll plaza and realizes he does not want to go through
     the toll lanes. He approaches BTO Bolton at Post B and
     indicates he is lost and needs to go to 11th Street and
     David Avenue. BTO Bolton gives the motorist the direc-
     tions from Post B.
     Which one of the following is the SHORTEST route for the
     motorist to take making sure to obey all traffic regula-
     tions?
     Travel east on 51st Avenue, then
          A. south on 12th Street, then west on Robert Overpass,
             then north on Francine Avenue, then east on John
             Avenue, then north on 11th Street to David Avenue
          B. north on 12th Street, then west on David Avenue to
             11th Street

    C. north on 12th Street, then west on Henry Avenue, then
       north on 11th Street to David Avenue
    D. south on 12th Street, then west on Robert Overpass,
       then north on Francine Avenue, then southeast on Lola
       Avenue, then north on 11th Street to David Avenue

17. In order for a Bridge and Tunnel Officer to determine   17.___
the classification of a vehicle, a BTO should follow
the procedure in the order given:
    I. Count the number of axles on the vehicle
   II. See if the vehicle's license plate is marked
     commercial or *passenger*
 III. Ask the driver for the weight of the vehicle
  IV. If there is uncertainty of the weight, request vehicle
    registration form and check it for weight
   V. If the registration form is unavailable, check the
    weight marking on the inside door panel of the vehicle
A van arrives in BTO Calvin's toll lane. BTO Calvin notices
that the van has two axles and commercial license plates.
The driver, when asked, is unaware of the vehicle's weight.
BTO Calvin should NEXT
    A. request vehicle registration form and check for the
      weight
    B. look inside the door of the vehicle for the weight
      marking
    C. estimate the weight by comparing it to previous vans
      of similar style
    D. check the vehicle's registration sticker for the
      weight

Questions 18-19.

DIRECTIONS: Questions 18 and 19 are to be answered SOLELY on the
            basis of the following information.

Bridge and Tunnel Officers are sometimes called upon to assist
an individual who is upset, or involved in an accident where injury
may have occurred. BTOs need to assist upset individuals who may
cause harm to themselves or others.

18. Which one of the following BEST describes a motorist in   18.___
need of assistance?
A motorist is
    A. involved in a minor car accident and is waiting in
      the car for assistance to arrive
    B. visibly angry about waiting in line for 15 minutes to
      pay the toll
    C. involved in a minor car accident on the bridge and
      is pacing alongside the vehicle
    D. sitting in a car with two crying children in the
      back seat

19. Which one of the following BEST describes a motorist in   19.___
    need of assistance?
    A(n)
       A. motorist who is lost and enters the toll plaza by
          mistake
       B. angry motorist who claims he was shortchanged by a BTO
       C. motorist walking in the tunnel because his pet got out
          of the family car in the tunnel
       D. motorist complaining because the gate in an automatic
          lane is stuck

Questions 20-22.

DIRECTIONS: Questions 20 through 22 are to be answered SOLELY on
             the basis of the following passage.

While assigned to *A* Post at the Metro Tunnel, Bridge and Tunnel
Officer Hunt observes a three vehicle accident involving two passenger
cars and a delivery truck. BTO Hunt responds to the accident scene
in a Ford patrol car and calls for assistance on his portable radio.
BTOs Pierce, Hunnicut, and Bendix are dispatched by Sgt. Baker. When
the three BTOs arrive at *A* Post, they see that the accident is minor.
One of the officers returns to tell Sgt. Baker that no emergency
vehicles or ambulances will be necessary. The three other BTOs
remain. Officers Bendix and Pierce begin to direct traffic around
the accident scene while Officer Hunt gathers the information needed
for an accident report.

Officer Hunt gathers the following information at the accident
scene: Vehicle One, a 1979 Chevrolet driven by Mr. Harrison Elliot;
Vehicle Two, a 1984 Honda Accord driven by Ms. Rhonda Meyers;
Vehicle Three, a 1976 GMC truck driven by Mr. Roscoe Goode. Based
on the information obtained, the GMC truck was in the center lane.
The accident occurred when the Chevrolet cut in front of the truck
from the right lane, causing the truck to swerve into the left lane,
hitting the Honda Accord. The Accord then spun into the center
lane and collided with the Chevrolet.

20. The FIRST officer to reach the accident scene was   20.___
       A. Hunt   B. Bendix   C. Hunnicut   D. Baker

21. The officer who went to report to the Sergeant was   21.___
       A. Hunt   B. Pierce   C. Bendix   D. Hunnicut

22. From the accident description, the accident was MOST   22.___
    likely started by the
       A. Accord swerving into the truck
       B. truck colliding with the Chevrolet
       C. Chevrolet changing lanes
       D. Ford colliding with the truck

23. *Bridge and Tunnel Officers sometimes rely on eyewitness accounts of incidents, even though eyewitnesses may make mistakes with regard to some details.*
Bridge and Tunnel Officer Franklin responds to a hit and run accident on the Jefferson Bridge. When she arrives, witnesses report four license plate numbers of the car that left the scene.
Which one of the following license numbers should BTO Franklin consider MOST likely to be correct?
    A. NFW-673   B. WFP-573   C. WPP-572   D. WFP-543

23.____

24. Bridge and Tunnel Officer Marx is investigating a motorist's complaint and has obtained the following information:

24.____

Place of Occurrence:	Henry Smith Bridge, Lane 7
Time of Occurrence:	Between 10:15 A.M. and 10:45 A.M.
Motorist:	Mr. Harold Rose
Time Reported:	11:15 A.M.
BTO Involved:	Unknown
Complaint:	Motorist was shortchanged

BTO Marx is completing a report on the incident.
Which one of the following expresses the above information MOST clearly and accurately?
    A. At 11:15 A.M., Mr. Harold Rose reported that he was shortchanged at the Henry Smith Bridge, Lane 7, between 10:15 A.M. and 10:45 A.M. by a BTO whose identity was unknown.
    B. Mr. Harold Rose reported between 10:15 A.M. and 10:45 A.M. he was shortchanged at 11:15 A.M. in Lane 7 of the Henry Smith Bridge by an unknown BTO.
    C. A BTO, whose identity was unknown, reported Mr. Harold Rose shortchanged him between 10:15 A.M. and 10:45 A.M. at the Henry Smith Bridge, Lane 7. He stated this at 11:15 A.M.
    D. At the Henry Smith Bridge, Lane 7, 11:15 A.M., Mr. Harold Rose, between 10:15 A.M. and 10:45 A.M., reported he was shortchanged by an unknown BTO.

25. *Bridge and Tunnel Officers are required to testify in court regarding summonses they have issued or arrests they have made.*
The following information relates to an arrest made by BTO Evans:

25.____

Date of Occurrence:	June 17, 1987
Time of Occurrence:	3:30 A.M.
Place of Occurrence:	Campus Street Bridge
Driver:	Claude Jones
Vehicle:	1974 Dodge Dart
Charges:	Driving While Intoxicated
Other Vehicle Involved:	1979 Ford pickup truck
Damage:	Dent in rear bumper of the 1979 Ford pickup truck

BTO Evans is testifying in court regarding this arrest. Which one of the following expresses the above information MOST clearly and accurately?

A. I arrested Claude Jones for driving a 1974 Dodge Dart intoxicated. He then drove his vehicle into the back of a 1979 Ford pickup truck, denting the bumper. This occurred at 3:30 A.M. on June 17, 1987, on the Campus Street Bridge.

B. At 3:30 A.M., on June 17, 1987, I arrested Claude Jones for driving while intoxicated on the Campus Street Bridge. He drove his 1974 Dodge Dart into the back of a 1979 Ford pickup truck, denting the truck's bumper.

C. At 3:30 A.M., I arrested Claude Jones for driving his 1974 Dodge Dart into the rear of a 1979 pickup truck, denting the bumper, while the driver was intoxicated on June 17, 1987, on the Campus Street Bridge.

D. On the Campus Street Bridge, I arrested Claude Jones for driving while intoxicated when an accident occurred between his 1974 Dodge Dart and a 1979 Ford pickup truck, denting the bumper at 3:30 A.M. on June 17, 1987

KEY (CORRECT ANSWERS)

1. B			11. C	
2. A			12. C	
3. B			13. D	
4. D			14. A	
5. D			15. B	
6. C			16. D	
7. A			17. A	
8. C			18. C	
9. B			19. C	
10. A			20. A	

21. D
22. C
23. B
24. A
25. B

EXAMINATION SECTION

TEST 1

DIRECTIONS: Each question or incomplete statement is followed by several suggested answers or completions. Select the one that BEST answers the question or completes the statement. *PRINT THE LETTER OF THE CORRECT ANSWER IN THE SPACE AT THE RIGHT.*

Questions 1-3.

DIRECTIONS: Questions 1 through 3 are to be answered SOLELY on the basis of the following passage.

Bridge and Tunnel Officer Frankel is assigned to Post 33 inside the Main Street Tunnel. All posts in the northbound tunnel are numbered using odd numbers. All posts in the southbound tunnel are numbered with even numbers. The sergeant on duty, Sgt. Hanks, drives through the northbound tunnel at 10:30 P.M. to check on the tunnel posts before taking his meal break. When he reaches BTO Frankel, Sgt. Hanks stops the patrol car and exits from his car in order to speak with Frankel. He informs the BTO that at 11:05 P.M. a truck with a wide load is expected to pass through the tunnel. BTO Frankel states he will be prepared for the vehicle and will watch for it.

Sgt. Hanks gets back into his patrol car and continues on his way to inform the other three officers in the northbound tunnel. At 10:50 P.M., Sgt. Hanks is heading to the facility building when his patrol car stalls in front of Post 44. BTO Torrey, stationed at the post, observes the disabled patrol car and leaves his post in order to assist the sergeant. Sgt. Hanks orders BTO Torrey to call for a wrecker to remove the patrol car from the tunnel.

1. At what post did Sgt. Hank's patrol car break down? Post
   A. 34, Northbound   B. 44, Southbound
   C. 43, Northbound   D. 33, Southbound

     1.____

2. How many BTOs were posted in the northbound tunnel?
   A. 2   B. 3   C. 4   D. 5

     2.____

3. Sgt. Hanks was driving through the northbound tunnel in order to
   A. inform the posts of the *wide load* truck
   B. find where BTO Frankel was stationed
   C. check on the tunnel posts
   D. return to the facility building

     3.____

4. *Bridge and Tunnel Officers sometimes rely on eyewitness accounts of incidents, even though eyewitnesses may make mistakes with regard to some details.*
   While assigned to Toll Lane 5, Bridge and Tunnel Officer Williams is approached by a motorist who states he saw a man driving on the expressway and waving a gun at other

     4.____

motorists. Three additional vehicles pull into Lanes 6, 7, and 8 and tell the BTOs assigned to those lanes that they also witnessed the man with a gun. The following are descriptions of the man and vehicle given by the four witnesses.
Which one of these descriptions should the BTOs consider MOST likely to be correct?
   A. White male, early twenties, white Cadillac
   B. Black male, between 20-25, white Lincoln
   C. White male, 30-40 years old, white Cadillac
   D. White male, around 25 years old, beige Chevrolet

5. While on tow truck duty, Bridge and Tunnel Officer McNeil   5.___
   responded to an accident and obtained the following information at the scene:

Place of Occurrence:	Lamppost, York Ave. Bridge
Time of Occurrence:	2:25 A.M.
Make and License No. of Car:	Dodge, license no. 427-ABM
Cause of Accident:	Wet roadway
Action Taken:	Hoisted and towed vehicle to disabled area of bridge

   BTO McNeil is completing an accident report.
   Which one of the following expresses the above information MOST clearly and accurately?
   A. On a wet roadway, a vehicle struck a lamppost and was hoisted and towed to a disabled area. The Dodge, license no. 427-ABM, was on the York Avenue Bridge at 2:25 A.M.
   B. A Dodge, license no. 427-ABM, drove into a lamppost on the York Avenue Bridge due to a wet roadway that had to be hoisted and towed off of the bridge at 2:25 A.M.
   C. A Dodge, license no. 427-ABM, drove into a lamppost at 2:25 A.M. on the York Avenue Bridge due to a wet roadway. The car was hoisted and towed off the bridge to the disabled area.
   D. A Dodge, license no. 427-ABM, hoisted and towed to a disabled area after 2:25 A.M. when it drove into a lamppost on the wet roadway of the York Avenue Bridge.

6. A convoy of tractor-trailers approaches Toll Lane 15,   6.___
   operated by Bridge and Tunnel Officer Watson. The driver
   of the first vehicle informs BTO Watson that he will pay
   for all vehicles in his convoy. Below is a list of the
   vehicles in the convoy.

No. of Vehicles	Class No.	Toll for the Vehicle Class
6	4	$2.00
4	5	$3.25
5	6	$3.75

In order for BTO Watson to calculate the toll amount for the convoy, which one of the following formulas should he use?

A. (6×4×5) + ($2.00×$3.25×$3.75)
B. (6×$2.00) + (4×$3.25) + (5×$3.75)
C. (4×$2.00) + (5×$3.25) + (6×$3.75)
D. (6+4+5) × ($2.00 + $3.25 + $3.75)

7. On February 15, 1988, Joyce Wright arrived at the facility building of the Army Memorial Bridge to file a complaint about being short-changed. Details of the incident are listed below:

Date Reported:	February 15, 1988
Date of Occurrence:	February 14, 1988
Time of Occurrence:	8:20 A.M.
Lane:	7
Direction Traveling:	West
Amount of Toll:	$1.50
Amount Given:	$20.00 bill
Change Returned:	$8.50

Bridge and Tunnel Officer Sanford is completing a report on the incident.

Which one of the following expresses the above information MOST clearly and accurately?

A. On February 15, 1988, Joyce Wright reported in Lane 7 that she was given only $8.50 for change when she paid the $1.50 toll with a $20.00 bill while traveling west on February 14, 1988 at 8:20 A.M.
B. On February 15, 1988, while traveling west, Joyce Wright reported at 8:20 A.M. she was shortchanged on February 14, 1988. She paid $20.00 for a $1.50 toll. She received $8.50 in Lane 7.
C. On February 15, 1988, Joyce Wright reported that she was shortchanged on February 14, 1988 at 8:20 A.M. in Lane 7 while traveling westbound. She received $8.50 in change after paying the $1.50 toll with a $20.00 bill.
D. Joyce Wright reported on February 14, 1988 she was shortchanged in westbound Lane 7 at 8:20 A.M. She paid the toll with a $20.00 bill and received $8.50 in change for the $1.50 toll according to the complainant on February 15, 1988.

8. *If a bill given to pay a toll is foreign or damaged currency, a Bridge and Tunnel Officer should not accept the money and request proper currency for payment of the toll. If the driver refuses, the BTO should call for a supervisor. When money given for a toll appears to be counterfeit, the BTO must request that the driver pull over to the side of the toll plaza and call a supervisor to question the driver.*

In which one of the following situations would a BTO MOST likely call for a supervisor?
A driver
   A. throws the toll payment at the BTO, then drives on
   B. uses a Canadian $5 bill to pay the toll
   C. gives a badly torn $5 bill and refuses to exchange the money for another bill
   D. hands the BTO a $5 bill that is off-color and wrinkled

Questions 9-11.

DIRECTIONS: Questions 9 through 11 are to be answered SOLELY on the basis of the following passage.

At 6:45 P.M., two motorists were involved in a minor accident on the toll plaza at the Cross-Bay Bridge. Tempers became short, and soon the two motorists were involved in a heated argument.

Bridge and Tunnel Officers Bender and Rourke, who were to start their tour at 6:50 P.M., arrived and broke up the altercation. The two drivers were separated and calmed. Each began to describe the accident to the officers.

Nicholas Warren informed Officer Rourke that he paid his toll in Lane 1, which is the extreme right lane. He wanted to go into the left lane on the bridge and began to move his vehicle to the left when his vehicle was struck in the rear by a vehicle leaving Toll Lane 2.

Olga Miller informed Officer Bender that she had paid her toll and was leaving Lane 2 when Mr. Warren's vehicle cut directly in front of her vehicle and caused the accident.

Ten minutes after the accident occurred, BTOs Pena and Bickford rang their supervisor and asked when they were to be relieved since their tours were scheduled to end at 7:00 P.M. Sergeant White explained to the two officers that their relief officers were taking information on an accident. Officers Pena and Bickford told the Sergeant that they would take over for Bender and Rourke and finish taking the information. Sgt. White approved the switch. Twenty-five minutes after the accident, all information was taken, and all parties left the scene.

9. Ms. Miller FIRST spoke to Officer   9.___
      A. Bender   B. Bickford   C. White   D. Pena

10. Officer Pena was due to end his tour at _____ P.M.   10.___
      A. 6:45   B. 6:50   C. 7:00   D. 7:10

11. In what toll lane did Mr. Warren pay the toll?   11.___
      A. 1   B. 2   C. 3   D. 4

12. Bridge and Tunnel Officer White is posted at the entrance 12.___
    to a tunnel. One of his responsibilities is to stop and
    reroute any vehicles that are dangerous or unsafe, such as
    a vehicle that is likely to endanger persons or property
    or make bridges or tunnels unsafe.
    BTO White would MOST likely reroute which one of the
    following vehicles?
    A
    A. cement truck which spills water down its side when it
       hits a bump
    B. tractor-trailer dragging one of its tie-down chains
    C. garbage truck with two helpers hanging on its back
       hopper
    D. moving van with its tailgate up and with furniture
       tied onto it

13. While assigned to Toll Lane 3, BTO Johnson sees a convoy 13.___
    of military vehicles approaching the toll plaza. Capt.
    Hernandez, the driver of the first vehicle, tells BTO
    Johnson that he will pay for all of the vehicles in the
    convoy. Capt. Hernandez gives BTO Johnson the following
    for payment of the toll:
         2 prepaid tickets at $2.00 each
         3 prepaid tickets at $3.75 each
         1 $50.00 bill
    Which one of the following methods should BTO Johnson use
    to determine how much payment he was given?
    A. Multiply the two tickets by $2.00, then multiply the
       three tickets by $3.75, then add those amounts to
       $50.00.
    B. Add the number of tickets and bills, then add the two
       ticket amounts, then multiply the two amounts, then add
       $50.00.
    C. Multiply one by $2.00, then multiply two by $3.75,
       then multiply three by $50.00, then add the three
       amounts.
    D. Multiply the two tickets by $2.00, then multiply the
       three tickets by $3.75, then add the sums.

Questions 14-15.

DIRECTIONS: Questions 14 and 15 are to be answered SOLELY on the
              basis of the following information.

    Bridge and Tunnel Officer Wendell is assigned to a toll plaza
post at the Wilson Bridge. At about 2:15 P.M., he observes John
Edwards drive into the toll lane without throwing any money into
the Exact Coin Machine. As BTO Wendell approaches the vehicle, Mr.
Edwards starts to blow his horn. BTO Wendell instructs Mr. Edwards
to place the proper toll into the machine, but Mr. Edwards refuses,
stating that the bridge toll is unfair. When BTO Wendell requests
Mr. Edwards' driver's license and car registration, Mr. Edwards
starts to yell and use abusive language. BTO Wendell warns Mr.
Edwards that he will be arrested if he continues to block the toll
lane. Mr. Edwards continues to yell, refuses to leave the lane,
and is arrested by BTO Wendell.

14. Officer Wendell FIRST observed Mr. Edwards when he   14.___
    A. started blowing his horn
    B. refused to leave the toll lane
    C. entered the toll lane
    D. began yelling and using abusive language

15. BTO Wendell arrested Mr. Edwards because he   15.___
    A. refused to pay the toll
    B. was yelling and using abusive language
    C. refused to give his license and registration to
       Officer Wendell
    D. was blocking the toll lane

Questions 16-18.

DIRECTIONS: Questions 16 through 18 are to be answered SOLELY on
               the basis of the following map. The flow of traffic is
               indicated by the arrows. If there is only one arrow
               shown, then traffic flows only in the direction indicated
               by the arrow. If there are two arrows, then traffic flows
               in both directions. You must follow the flow of traffic.

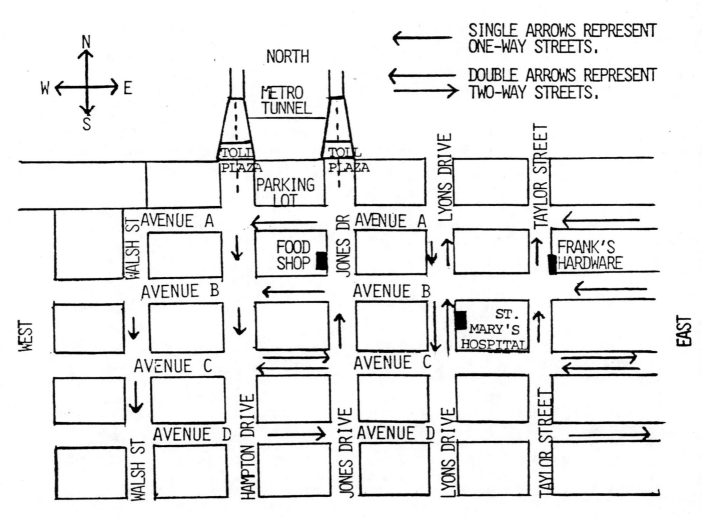

16. A motorist is exiting the Metro Tunnel and approaches the
    bridge and tunnel officer at the toll plaza. He asks the
    BTO how to get to the food shop on Jones Drive.
    Which one of the following is the SHORTEST route for the
    motorist to take, making sure to obey all traffic regula-
    tions?
    Travel south on Hampton Drive, then left on _____ on Jones
    Drive to the food shop.
       A. Avenue A, then right   B. Avenue B, then right
       C. Avenue D, then left   D. Avenue C, then left

    16._____

17. A motorist heading south pulls up to a toll booth at the
    exit of the Metro Tunnel and asks BTO Evans how to get
    to Frank's Hardware Store on Taylor Street.
    Which one of the following is the SHORTEST route for the
    motorist to take, making sure to obey all traffic regula-
    tions?
    Travel south on Hampton Drive, then east on
       A. Avenue B to Taylor Street
       B. Avenue D, then north on Taylor Street to Avenue B
       C. Avenue C, then north on Taylor Street to Avenue B
       D. Avenue C, then north on Lyons Drive, then east on
          Avenue B to Taylor Street

    17._____

18. A motorist is exiting the Metro Tunnel and approaches
    the toll plaza. She asks BTO Owens for directions to St.
    Mary's Hospital.
    Which one of the following is the SHORTEST route for the
    motorist to take, making sure to obey all traffic regula-
    tions?
    Travel south on Hampton Drive, then _____ on Lyons Drive
    to St. Mary's Hospital.
       A. left on Avenue D, then left
       B. right on Avenue A, then left on Walsh Street, then
          left on Avenue D, then left
       C. left on Avenue C, then left
       D. left on Avenue B, then right

    18._____

19. While on duty at a bridge toll plaza, Bridge and Tunnel
    Officer White was told by a motorist that she realized
    she was off her intended route and was going the wrong
    way. The woman did not want to pay the toll or go over
    the bridge. Officer White recorded the following informa-
    tion:

    19._____

          Toll Lane: 10
          License Plate Number: 627-AIB
          Make of Car: Ford
          Motorist's Name: Joan Semoore
          Number of Occupants: Three
          Time of Occurrence: 10:27 A.M.

    Officer White is completing an Off-Route report on this
    incident.

Which one of the following expresses the above information MOST clearly and accurately?
   A. Joan Semoore was off-route in a Ford in Lane 10, license plate number 627-AIB, at 10:27 A.M., with three occupants.
   B. At 10:27 A.M., a Ford, license plate number 627-AIB, was off-route with Joan Semoore and three occupants in Lane 10.
   C. At 10:27 A.M., a Ford, license plate number 627-AIB, driven by Joan Semoore, was off-route in Lane 10. There were three occupants in the car.
   D. Joan Semoore drove three occupants and a Ford, license plate number 627-AIB, off-route in Lane 10, at 10:27 A.M.

20. When wind speeds reach high levels, Bridge and Tunnel Officers are required to restrict some vehicles from the bridges.
When winds are over 30 mph, the following vehicles are restricted:
   1. House trailers
   2. Vehicles transporting plate glass, large signs, or similar objects
   3. Empty tractor trailers
When winds are over 40 mph, the above vehicles are restricted as well as the vehicles listed below:
   1. Motorcycles
   2. Trailers carrying boats or cars
   3. Vehicles dangerously loaded
Which one of the following BEST describes a vehicle that would be restricted when the wind is 35 mph?
A
   A. tractor trailer transporting new automobiles
   B. truck carrying long iron beams
   C. motorcycle
   D. tractor trailer delivering a 12 foot sign to a restaurant

20.___

Questions 21-22.

DIRECTIONS: Questions 21 and 22 are to be answered SOLELY on the basis of the following information.

After the completion of a tour of duty, a Bridge and Tunnel Officer is required to tally and total all paper currency (bills) collected during his tour and submit a Cash Deposit Report. This report lists the bills by denomination, the number of bills, and the total amount for each denomination.

Note that each line on this form is lettered from A to F for your reference.

	Denomination	Number of Bills	Total Amount of Cash
A	100	8	$800
B	50		$550
C	20	177	
D	10	46	
E	5		$245
F	1	1011	

21. The TOTAL amount of cash on Line C should be
    A. $3400　　　B. $3440　　　C. $3540　　　D. $3600

21.＿＿

22. What is the number of $5 bills that should be entered in
    Line E?
    A. 47　　　B. 48　　　C. 49　　　D. 54

22.＿＿

23. Bridge and Tunnel Officers are occasionally called upon
    to administer emergency first aid to seriously injured
    persons. BTO Williams, assigned to one of the emergency
    tractors, has just arrived at the scene of a two-car
    accident on the plaza.
    Which one of the following individuals should be the FIRST
    to receive first aid from BTO Williams?
    The
    A. passenger in the first car is complaining of a bruised
       knee
    B. driver in the second car is suffering an apparent heart
       attack
    C. driver in the first car is bleeding heavily from the
       nose
    D. passenger in the second car has a broken arm

23.＿＿

24. Bridge and Tunnel Officer Franklin has just finished
    investigating an accident on a bridge and has obtained
    the following information:

    Place of Occurrence:　　Midspan of the bridge
    Time of Occurrence:　　11:20 P.M.
    Driver of Vehicle:　　John Thomas
    Accident Description:　　Vehicle hit the guard rail
    Action Taken:　　Vehicle was towed and the driver
    　　　　　　　　　was held for driving while intoxi-
    　　　　　　　　　cated

    BTO Franklin is describing the occurrence to Sergeant
    Wilson.
    Which one of the following expresses the above information
    MOST clearly and accurately?
    A. Upon investigation at the midspan of the bridge at
       11:20 P.M., John Thomas' vehicle was towed after it
       hit the guard rail while driving intoxicated. It
       was held.
    B. At the midspan of the bridge, I investigated an acci-
       dent where John Thomas, driving while intoxicated,
       at 11:20 P.M., drove his vehicle into the guard rail.
       His vehicle was towed and was held.

24.＿＿

C. At 11:20 P.M., John Thomas, driving while intoxicated, drove his vehicle into the guard rail at the midspan of the bridge. After I investigated the accident, the vehicle was towed. John Thomas is being held.

D. At 11:20 P.M., I investigated John Thomas being held for driving his vehicle while intoxicated into the midspan guard rail of the bridge. The vehicle was towed from the accident.

25. Bridge and Tunnel Officer Storm is collecting tolls in Lane 7 of the Miller Bridge. A group of vehicles arrive in his lane in a single line. The driver of the first vehicle hands the following list to BTO Storm: 2 cars - Class 1; 3 vans - Class 2; 1 truck - Class 4; 2 cars with trailers - Class 5.

Vehicle Class	Toll Amount
Class 1	$1.00
Class 2	$1.50
Class 4	$2.25
Class 5	$3.00

In order for BTO Storm to determine the CORRECT toll amount to collect from the driver, he should

A. add the number of vehicles in each class to the toll amount for the class, then add the four amounts together

B. add the number of vehicles, then add the amounts of toll per class, then multiply the two amounts together

C. multiply one x $1.00, then multiply two x $1.50, then multiply four x $2.25, then multiply five x $3.00, then add the four amounts together

D. multiply two x $1.00, then multiply three x $1.50, then multiply one x $2.25, then multiply two x $3.00, then add those amounts

25.___

KEY (CORRECT ANSWERS)

1. B	11. A
2. C	12. C
3. A/C	13. A
4. A	14. C
5. C	15. D
6. B	16. D
7. C	17. C
8. C	18. C
9. A	19. C
10. C	20. D

21. C
22. C
23. B
24. C
25. D

TEST 2

1. Bridge and Tunnel Officer Grummund responds to an accident and obtains the following information:

Place of Occurrence:	Andrea Bridge
Number of Vehicles Involved:	Three
Type of Accident:	Rear-end collision
Number of Injured:	Four
Direction of Travel:	Southbound
Witness:	Mrs. Angela Court

    BTO Grummund is reporting the accident to the Sergeant. Which one of the following expresses the above information MOST clearly and accurately?
    A. At the Andrea Bridge, three vehicles had a rear-end collision accident with four injuries, reported Mrs. Angela Court.
    B. At the Andrea Bridge, three vehicles were involved in a rear-end collision accident. This information, obtained by Mrs. Angela Court, included four injured.
    C. Southbound on the Andrea Bridge, three vehicles were involved in a rear-end collision involving four injuries and witnessed by Mrs. Angela Court.
    D. At the Andrea Bridge, three vehicles were involved in a rear-end collision resulting in four injuries. The accident occurred in the southbound roadway and was witnessed by Mrs. Angela Court.

1.___

Questions 2-3.

DIRECTIONS: Questions 2 and 3 are to be answered SOLELY on the basis of the following information.

Bridge and Tunnel Officers are responsible for observing and stopping vehicles that are considered hazards to themselves, to other vehicles, or to the bridge or tunnel.

2. Which one of the following vehicles would a BTO MOST likely prohibit from using a bridge or tunnel?
    A
    A. station wagon with bicycles tied to the roof rack
    B. pick-up truck pulling a tractor on a trailer
    C. garbage truck with debris falling out of the back
    D. truck hauling telephone poles with a red flag tied to the end of the poles

2.___

3. Which one of the following vehicles would a BTO MOST   3.___
   likely allow to use a bridge or tunnel?
   A
      A. pick-up truck with boards extending 5 feet over the
         left side
      B. fuel oil truck leaking oil from the storage tank
      C. garbage truck with smoke coming from its garbage bin
      D. flatbed truck with barrels strapped down to the
         trailer bed

Questions 4-8.

DIRECTIONS: Questions 4 through 8 are to be answered SOLELY on
              the basis of the following information.

   Bridge and Tunnel Officers must calculate the correct change to
return to a motorist.

   Assume that the toll for each vehicle is $1.75. Determine the
correct amount of change that should be returned to the driver for
the following transactions.

4. A $20.00 bill is given to pay the toll for one vehicle.   4.___
   The change returned should be
      A. $18.25   B. $18.75   C. $19.25   D. $19.75

5. A $20.00 bill is given to pay the toll for three vehicles.   5.___
   The change returned should be
      A. $14.75   B. $15.25   C. $15.75   D. $18.25

6. A $5.00 bill is given to pay the toll for one vehicle.   6.___
   The change returned should be
      A. $2.50   B. $2.75   C. $3.00   D. $3.25

7. A $50.00 bill is given to pay the toll for ten vehicles.   7.___
   The change returned should be
      A. $25.00   B. $30.50   C. $32.50   D. $42.50

8. A $10.00 bill is given for payment of toll for six vehicles. 8.___
   The Bridge and Tunnel Officer should next
      A. return $6.50 to the driver
      B. return $1.75 to the driver
      C. ask the driver for an additional fifty cents
      D. allow the vehicles to go through since the toll is
         paid in full

9. At 4:40 P.M., Bridge and Tunnel Officer Rasmon responds   9.___
   to the scene of an accident. The following information
   was obtained by the BTO:

         Vehicles Involved: 1981 Ford
                                   1979 GMC truck
                                   1978 Volkswagon
         Time of Occurrence: 4:35 P.M.
         Place of Occurrence: Brownsville Bridge
         Vehicle Needing a Tow: 1981 Ford
         Witness: Sheila Norris

BTO Rasmon is reporting this information to the sergeant on duty.
Which one of the following expresses the above information MOST clearly and accurately?

    A. Sheila Norris reported at 4:35 P.M. she witnessed an accident involving a 1981 Ford, which needed to be towed, a 1979 GMC truck, and a 1978 Volkswagon on the Brownsville Bridge. I responded to the scene at 4:40 P.M.

    B. At 4:40 P.M., I responded to an accident on the Brownsville Bridge. The accident occurred at 4:35 P.M. and was witnessed by Sheila Norris. A 1981 Ford, a 1979 GMC truck, and a 1978 Volkswagon were involved in the accident. A tow was required for the 1981 Ford.

    C. I responded to an accident on the Brownsville Bridge at 4:40 P.M. A 1981 Ford needed a tow, as well as a 1979 GMC truck, and a 1978 Volkswagon, which were involved in the accident witnessed by Sheila Norris at 4:35 P.M.

    D. I responded at 4:40 P.M. to an accident with a 1979 GMC truck, a 1981 Ford that needed a tow, and a 1978 Volkswagon that was witnessed by Sheila Norris at 4:35 P.M.

10. Bridge and Tunnel Officers are required to put automatic toll lanes into operation. BTOs should do the following in the order given:

    1. Insert the coin box in the toll collecting machine and lock it
    2. Insert the Sergeant's identification key in the register, take a reading, and withdraw the key
    3. Insert the operating identification key in the register for the length of the tour
    4. Open the barrier of the toll lane

BTO Higgens has been directed to open the automatic toll lane. He has inserted the coin box in the toll collecting machine, locked it, and inserted the Sergeant's identification key in the register.
BTO Higgens should next

    A. take a reading and withdraw the key from the register
    B. insert the operating identification key in the register for the length of the tour
    C. open the barrier to allow traffic to use the lane
    D. insert the Sergeant's identification key in the register

10.___

11. While collecting tolls at the Whitehouse Bridge, Bridge and Tunnel Officer Smith observed a vehicle pass through his toll lane without paying the toll. The following details were obtained by BTO Smith:

11.___

Vehicle Year and Make:	1985 Ford
Vehicle Color:	Black
License Plate Number:	BIX-621, New York
Driver Description:	Male, White, Blonde Hair
Time of Occurrence:	8:50 A.M.
Place of Occurrence:	Toll Lane 6

BTO Smith is completing a report on the situation.
Which one of the following expresses the above information
MOST clearly and accurately?

A. Toll Lane 6 was not payed a toll by a black Ford, New York license plate number BIX-621. A White male, driving the 1985 vehicle at 8:50 A.M., had blonde hair.

B. A White male did not stop at Toll Lane 6. The blonde-haired driver of a black 1985 Ford did not pay the toll at 8:50 A.M. He was driving with New York plates, license number BIX-621.

C. At 8:50 A.M., a White male with blonde hair failed to pay the toll in Lane 6. He was driving a black 1985 Ford with New York license plates BIX-621.

D. Driving a black 1985 Ford at 8:50 A.M., a White male with blonde hair did not stop in Toll Lane 6. His black 1985 Ford with New York plates BIX-621 failed to pay the toll.

12. Bridge and Tunnel Officers are required to assist disabled vehicles in the tunnel. When a car has stalled in the tunnel, the BTO assigned to the nearest tunnel booth should do the following in the order given:

1. Go to the nearest Signal Control Station.
2. Press the amber light button.
3. Press the emergency truck button to notify the wrecker driver.
4. Go to the disabled vehicle and direct traffic around the car.
5. When the wrecker is ready to pull the car out of the tunnel, go back to the Signal Control Station and press the green button.
6. Call the Desk Officer to inform him of the status of the flow of traffic.

BTO Wakeman is assigned to Signal Control Station 33 at the Near River tunnel. He notices that a car has stopped and has the hazard lights flashing. BTO Wakeman presses the amber light button at his Signal Control Station. He determines that the car is disabled and calls for a wrecker by pressing the emergency truck button. While the BTO is directing traffic, the wrecker arrives, attaches the car to the hoist, and is ready to remove the car from the tunnel. BTO Wakeman should next

A. call the Desk Officer to inform him of the wrecker's progress
B. return to the Signal Control Station and press the green button
C. continue to direct traffic until the wrecker has left the tunnel
D. return to the Signal Control Station and press the amber button

12.____

13. Bridge and Tunnel Officer Brown responds to an accident   13.___
    that occurred in the Northbound Tunnel. The following
    details were obtained at the scene:

        Place of Accident: 100 feet south of Tunnel
                                     Post 15
        Vehicles Involved: 1985 Volvo, 1984 Dodge,
                                     1983 Ford
        Number of Wreckers Needed: Two
        Time of Accident: 10:35 A.M.

    BTO Brown returns to Tunnel Post 15 and phones the Desk
    Officer to request the wreckers.
    Which one of the following expresses the above information
    MOST clearly and accurately?
        A. Three vehicles were involved 100 feet south of Tunnel
           Post 15 at 10:35 A.M. in an accident requiring two
           wreckers. A 1985 Volvo, a 1984 Dodge, and a 1983 Ford
           were in the Northbound Tunnel.
        B. Two wreckers are needed as a result of an accident
           that occurred at 10:35 A.M. in the Northbound Tunnel,
           100 feet south of Tunnel Post 15. The vehicles
           involved are a 1985 Volvo, a 1984 Dodge, and a 1983
           Ford.
        C. At 10:35 A.M., an accident occurred. A 1985 Volvo,
           a 1984 Dodge, and a 1983 Ford were 100 feet south of
           Tunnel Post 15 in the Northbound Tunnel, and two
           wreckers are needed.
        D. At 10:35 A.M., an accident occurred involving a 1985
           Volvo, a 1984 Dodge, and a 1983 Ford. Two wreckers
           are required 100 feet south of Tunnel Post 15 in the
           Northbound Tunnel.

14. Bridge and Tunnel Officers are required to inspect and   14.___
    drive the wrecker. At the beginning of their tour, all
    wrecker drivers should check each item listed below in
    the order given:
        1. Gas in tank
        2. Oil level
        3. Radiator liquid
        4. Lights (front, rear, brake, flashers, rotary)
        5. Tire pressure
        6. Fire extinguishers
        7. Fire tank (water and foam levels)
        8. Power take-off (operates hoist)
        9. Cleanliness
        10. Operation of the two-way radio
        11. First aid kits
    On Sunday, BTO Smith is assigned Wrecker #149 on his
    7 A.M. - 3 P.M. tour of duty. He begins to inspect the
    wrecker. He checks to see if he has enough fuel; he
    checks the oil level; he checks the radiator and all lights.
    BTO Smith is then called away from his wrecker.

When he returns, he should next check the
A. tire pressure
B. fire extinguishers
C. cleanliness of the vehicle
D. operation of the two-way radio

15. Bridge and Tunnel Officer Gallo has been called to court   15.___
to testify about two summonses he issued on December 4,
1987. BTO Gallo refers to his memo book entries on the
incident to prepare himself for the testimony. The
relevant memo book entries are listed below:

Date of Occurrence:	December 4, 1987
Time of Occurrence:	12:40 P.M.
Name of Driver:	Vincent Bourne
Vehicle Year and Make:	1986 Pontiac
Violations:	Uninspected vehicle, uninsured vehicle
Officer Assignment:	Post B

BTO Gallo must testify on the incident.
Which one of the following expresses the above information
MOST clearly and accurately?
A. On December 4, 1987, Vincent Bourne was driving at
12:40 P.M. The 1986 Pontiac was uninspected and unin-
sured. Summonses were issued while I was assigned to
Post B.
B. A 1986 Pontiac driven by Vincent Bourne received two
summonses for being uninsured and unregistered at
12:40 P.M. while I was assigned to Post B on
December 4, 1987.
C. While assigned to Post B on December 4, 1987, at
12:40 P.M., I issued two summonses to Vincent Bourne.
One of the summonses issued was for driving an
uninsured vehicle and the other was for driving an
unregistered vehicle. Vincent Bourne was driving a
1986 Pontiac.
D. On December 4, 1987, Vincent Bourne was issued two
summonses for driving a 1986 Pontiac at 12:40 P.M.
While I was assigned to Post B, he received them
for driving an uninsured and unregistered vehicle.

16. A Bridge and Tunnel Officer who makes an arrest should   16.___
do the following in the order given:
1. Handcuff the arrested person.
2. Search the person.
3. Read the arrested person his rights.
4. Escort the person to the local precinct and file
a complaint.
5. Verify if the arrested person is intoxicated by
administering a breath test.
6. Get an arrest number from Central Booking.

BTO Berry observes a vehicle swerving while approaching the toll plaza. He orders the vehicle to stop and observes the driver appearing drunk and tells the driver he is under arrest. After handcuffing the driver, searching him, and reading him his rights, BTO Berry escorts the driver to the 32nd Precinct.
BTO Berry should next
   A. take the prisoner's handcuffs off at the police precinct
   B. proceed to Central Booking for an arrest number
   C. administer a breath test to determine level of intoxication
   D. file a complaint at the police precinct

Questions 17-19.

DIRECTIONS: Questions 17 through 19 are to be answered SOLELY on the basis of the following information.

Class	Description of Vehicle
Class 1	A two-axle passenger car, van, or truck under 7,000 lbs.
Class 2	A Class 1 vehicle with a one-axle trailer or a three-axle mobile home
Class 3	A Class 1 vehicle with a two-axle trailer or a three-axle vehicle with a single-axle trailer
Class 4	A two-axle vehicle with a maximum weight over 7,000 lbs., a two-axle tractor, or a two-axle bus
Class 5	A public city-owned bus with two or three axles
Class 6	A four-axle truck or a private three-axle bus
Class 7	A motorcycle

17.   What is the CORRECT class of a van weighing 6,500 lbs.?   17.____
   A. 1   B. 2   C. 3   D. 4

18.   What is the CORRECT class of a private three-axle bus?   18.____
   A. 3   B. 4   C. 5   D. 6

19.   In order for a car to be considered a Class 3 vehicle,   19.____
it must have a weight
   A. under 7,000 lbs. and a two-axle trailer
   B. over 7,000 lbs. and a two-axle trailer
   C. under 7,000 lbs. and a three-axle trailer
   D. under 7,000 lbs. and a single-axle trailer

20.   While collecting tolls from 10:00 A.M. to 12:00 P.M.,   20.____
Bridge and Tunnel Officer Simpson observed a motorist lose control of his vehicle. Officer Simpson obtained the following details:

Time of Occurrence:	10:55 A.M.
Place of Occurrence:	In front of Toll Booth 6
Description of Incident:	Lost control of vehicle and drove into cement barrier
Vehicle:	1985 Oldsmobile
Driver:	Nick Flower
Damage:	Cracked cement barrier
Action Taken:	Summons issued for Reckless Driving

BTO Simpson is completing a report on the incident.
Which one of the following expresses the above information
MOST clearly and accurately?

A. Between 10:00 A.M. and 12:00 P.M., Nick Flower cracked the cement barrier with his 1985 Oldsmobile by driving into it after losing control. He was issued a summons for Reckless Driving while I was collecting tolls in Toll Booth 6 at 10:55 A.M.

B. While collecting tolls in Toll Booth 6 between 10:00 A.M. and 12:00 P.M., Nick Flower lost control of his 1985 Oldsmobile and drove into the cement barrier at Toll Booth 6, cracked it at 10:55 A.M., and was issued a summons for Reckless Driving.

C. At 10:55 A.M., Nick Flower lost control and cracked the cement barrier in front of Toll Booth 6 while driving into it with his 1985 Oldsmobile. He was issued a summons for Reckless Driving while I was collecting tolls between 10:00 A.M. and 12:00 P.M.

D. At 10:55 A.M., while I was collecting tolls between 10:00 A.M. and 12:00 P.M. in Toll Booth 6, Nick Flower lost control of his 1985 Oldsmobile. He drove into the cement barrier in front of Toll Booth 6 and cracked it. He was issued a summons for Reckless Driving.

Questions 21-22.

DIRECTIONS: Questions 21 and 22 are to be answered SOLELY on the basis of the following information.

Bridge and Tunnel Officers are required to sell rolls of tokens.

21. Bridge and Tunnel Officer Victor began collecting tolls   21.___
at 7:00 A.M. with 50 rolls of tokens. During his tour,
BTO Victor was issued 25 additional rolls of tokens three
times. When BTO Victor completed his toll collecting
assignment, he returned 13 rolls of tokens.
How many rolls of tokens did BTO Victor sell?
   A. 62   B. 112   C. 137   D. 138

22. BTO Smith was issued 100 rolls of tokens at the start of   22._____
    her toll collecting assignment. During her tour, she was
    given an additional 30 rolls of tokens. BTO Smith sold a
    total of 93 rolls of tokens.
    How many rolls of tokens did BTO Smith have at the end of
    her tour?
       A. 7   B. 34   C. 37   D. 39

Questions 23-24.

DIRECTIONS: Questions 23 and 24 are to be answered SOLELY on the
              basis of the following information.

Vehicle Class	Description
Class 1	A two-axle vehicle weighing under 7,000 lbs.
Class 2	A Class 1 vehicle with a one-axle trailer
Class 3	A Class 1 vehicle with a two-axle trailer
Class 4	A two-axle vehicle weighing over 7,000 lbs.
Class 5	A Class 4 vehicle with a one-axle trailer or a three-axle truck with commercial plates
Class 6	A Class 4 vehicle with a two-axle trailer
Class 7	A three-axle vehicle with non-commercial plates
Class 8	A four-axle vehicle

23. BTO Wilson notices a two-axle vehicle with a one-axle   23._____
    trailer arrive in her toll lane.
    In order for BTO Wilson to determine the toll class, she
    should
       A. check the vehicle's weight
       B. check if the vehicle is a commercial vehicle
       C. count the number of axles
       D. ask the driver for the trailer's weight

24. In order for a vehicle with a trailer to be a Class 6   24._____
    vehicle, the vehicle
       A. weight must be over 7,000 lbs., and the trailer must
          have two axles
       B. weight must be under 7,000 lbs., and the trailer must
          have two axles
       C. must have commercial plates, and the trailer must have
          two axles
       D. must be over 7,000 lbs., and the trailer must have
          one axle

25. When a Bridge and Tunnel Officer is working a toll lane   25._____
    and counterfeit or altered money is given for the toll,
    the BTO should do the following in the order given:
       1. Request that the motorist drive out of the lane to
          a safe location.
       2. Do not return the bill to the motorist.
       3. Note the motorist's description and the description
          of any passengers.

4. Obtain a description of the vehicle such as make and model and license plate number.
5. Write your initials and the date on the counterfeit bill.
6. Notify your supervisor.
7. If the car has left the lane, the BTO shall submit a Special Report of Unusual Occurrences.
8. Enclose counterfeit currency in an envelope.

BTO Becker is assigned to a toll lane for a 20 minute relief. Upon completion of his 20 minutes in the lane, he notices that what appears to be a $10.00 bill is actually a $1.00 bill with the corners changed from 1 to 10. He does not remember who gave the bill to him.
Officer Becker should next
  A. note the motorist's description
  B. note the license number and submit a Special Report of Unusual Occurrences
  C. enclose the bill in an envelope
  D. initial and date the bill

KEY (CORRECT ANSWERS)

1. C/D
2. C
3. D
4. A
5. A

6. D
7. C
8. C
9. B
10. A

11. C
12. B
13. B/D
14. A
15. A

16. D
17. A
18. D
19. A
20. D

21. B
22. C
23. A
24. A
25. D

EXAMINATION SECTION
TEST 1

DIRECTIONS: Each question or incomplete statement is followed by several suggested answers or completions. Select the one that BEST answers the question or completes the statement. *PRINT THE LETTER OF THE CORRECT ANSWER IN THE SPACE AT THE RIGHT.*

1. Bridge and tunnel officers are given first aid instruction as a part of their training.
   Of the following, which *one* is the MOST important reason for this training?
   A. It fosters a spirit of competition among the officers.
   B. Officers will be able to show their first aid card in an emergency.
   C. In case an officer is sick he will be able to treat himself without visiting a doctor.
   D. An officer may be in a situation where an injured person needs aid.

   1. ___

2. Suppose that, as a toll collector, you believe that a slightly different procedure from the one you have been told to use would save some time while performing one of your duties.
   Which one of the following would be the BEST thing for you to do?
   A. Speak to your supervisor about the new procedure and the reasons you believe it will be useful
   B. Forget your idea because supervisors usually do not like suggestions from lower-ranking employees
   C. Try the new procedure yourself for a while to see if it really will save some time
   D. Write a letter to a newspaper so that you will have some aid in trying to get your suggestion accepted

   2. ___

3. Assume that, as a bridge and tunnel officer, you are stationed at a tunnel toll booth where cars are required to pay $1.50 in tolls. A motorist hands you a $5.00 bill and you give him change but one of the coins rolls under his car.
   Of the following, the BEST thing for you to do is to
   A. have the motorist get out and reach under the car for the coin
   B. give the driver another coin and pick up the one he dropped after his car has passed through the toll lane
   C. walk out of the toll booth, reach under the car for the coin, and hand it to the motorist
   D. take the motorist's home address and send him the coin by mail

   3. ___

4. Assume that you are collecting tolls at a bridge and a   4.___
   motorist says to you: *When I was crossing the middle
   of the bridge I saw a man standing on the other side who
   looked like he was going to jump off.*
   Of the following, the FIRST thing you should do is to
   A. signal your supervisor and tell him what the motorist
      said
   B. leave your toll booth and rush to stop the man from
      jumping
   C. tell the motorist that rescuing the man is not one
      of your duties
   D. shout to the other officers collecting tolls and
      tell them to stop all traffic approaching the bridge

5. Suppose that a car stops a few feet beyond your toll booth   5.___
   making it impossible for you to collect the toll.
   The BEST action for you to take would be to
   A. tell the driver to back up in front of your booth
      and then drive up to the booth again
   B. report the driver to your supervisor for failing to
      obey authority regulations
   C. ask the driver to get out of the car and hand you
      the toll
   D. walk to the vehicle, take the toll, and return to
      your booth

6. An authority regulation states that officers must keep   6.___
   premises and equipment in a neat, clean and **sanitary**
   condition.
   Which *one* of the following is the BEST reason for this
   regulation?
   A. Motorists do not like to use facilities which are
      sloppy and dirty.
   B. Properly maintained equipment has a higher resale value.
   C. It permits a continuous reduction of costs through
      the elimination of sanitation employees.
   D. Dirty equipment may make tasks difficult and may be
      unsafe

7. An authority rule states that giving driving instructions   7.___
   in an automobile is prohibited on authority bridges and
   in tunnels.
   Of the following, which *one* is the *most likely* reason for this
   rule?
   A. A student driver may create hazardous conditions.
   B. The toll is an extra, unnecessary expense for the
      driver
   C. The student driver will not be able to practice
      making turns
   D. An officer may be tempted to spend time observing the
      student's driving.

8. While an officer is collecting tolls at a bridge, a motorist who apparently speaks little English stops at the toll booth. The motorist is confused about what to do. Of the following, which *one* would be the BEST action for the officer to take?
    A. Write out instructions to the motorist, because it is easier to understand a language when it is written than when it is spoken
    B. Use hand motions, pointing to the correct toll to be paid and showing the motorist which lane to use while driving over the bridge
    C. Let the motorist proceed over the bridge without paying a toll, since trying to explain what to do would cause an enormous traffic delay
    D. Find out what language the motorist speaks and then ask the other officers who are collecting tolls whether any of them speaks that language

8.___

9. Officers are often given various kinds of training courses.
These officers are *more* effective because they
    A. have greater earning power
    B. can advance sooner than other officers
    C. are aware of proper procedures
    D. speak better than untrained officers

9.___

10. Officers are instructed to write reports of unusual occurrences, and the way they handled them, during their tours of duty.
Of the following, the MAIN reason for this rule is to
    A. show how effectively the bridges and tunnels are being managed
    B. show that one method of reporting is as good as another
    C. provide an accurate record of such incidents
    D. give the officers practice in the kind of writing they will need to do if they are promoted

10.___

11. Suppose that an officer observes an accident involving two vehicles approaching the toll booths of a bridge. Of the following, which would be LEAST important for the officer to note in a report of the accident?
    A. Names of the drivers of the vehicles
    B. Number of vehicles backed up in the toll lanes
    C. Date and time of the accident
    D. Actions the officer took immediately after seeing the accident

11.___

12. An officer stops a vehicle for a traffic violation and   12. ___
     asks for the driver's license. Previous traffic viola-
     tions are listed on the license.
     Asking the driver questions about these violations is
        A. *right*, because it helps the officer in describing
           the present violation
        B. *right*, because it gives the officer an idea of the
           driver's character
        C. *wrong*, because previous entries should have no bear-
           ing on present violations
        D. *wrong*, because the officer and motorist may get
           involved in a friendly discussion

13. Officers assigned to a patrol post inside a tunnel should   13. ___
     be constantly on the alert, observing everything that
     takes place.
     Of the following, the MAIN reason for this rule is that
     officers will be *better* able to
        A. give summonses to motorists who are speeding or
           changing lanes
        B. detect possible criminals among the motorists or
           passengers
        C. show the public that they re reliable and hard
           working employees
        D. aid in maintaining the flow of traffic and detect
           any dangerous situations

14. At the end of a tour of duty collecting tolls, each offi-   14. ___
     cer must count and separately wrap each. of the various
     denominations of bills he has collected.
     Of the following, the BEST reason for following this proce-
     dure is that it
        A. is a valuable way for each officer to drill on
           arithmetic skills
        B. guarentees that each officer will be able to dis-
           cover any forged bills
        C. allows each officer to replace any small shortages
           of toll money with his own funds
        D. enables each officer to submit his money in an
           orderly manner

15. An officer at a toll booth sees that traffic in the   15. ___
     adjacent lane which has an automatic toll collecting
     machine, is blocked due to a car stalled near the
     machine.
     Which *one* of the following is the BEST action for the
     officer to take?
        A. Leave his toll booth and direct blocked traffic in-
           to other lanes
        B. Ignore the situation, since the drivers will even-
           tually realize what has happened and will move to
           another lane
        C. Quickly go to the stalled vehicle, ask the driver
           if he needs assistance and then return to the toll
           booth
        D. Stay in his booth, but notify his supervisor about
           the problem in the automobile toll lane

16. Suppose that, as a bridge and tunnel officer, you have   16.___
    been assigned to a shift which begins at 7:00 a.m.
    While driving to work you get caught in a traffic jam and
    will be at least an hour late for your shift.
    Which *one* of the following would be the BEST thing for
    you to do?
    A. Continue driving to work, but explain your lateness
       to your supervisor as soon as you see him
    B. Call your supervisor on the nearest available tele-
       phone and tell him what happened
    C. Return home and then notify your supervisor that you will
       not be coming to work that day
    D. Call another officer who is not assigned to the
       7:00 a.m. shift and tell him to take your place
       till you arrive

17. Suppose that, as a bridge and tunnel officer, you are   17.___
    collecting tolls at a tunnel and the traffic is heavy.
    An out-of-state motorist pays the toll and says that he
    needs directions to his destination. He seems upset,
    and starts to hand you a road map and a pencil while
    asking you to indicate the best route on the map.
    Of the following, the BEST action for you to take is to
    A. tell him that it is not your job to help people who
       are lost
    B. take his map and pencil and carefully detail the
       most direct route for him to follow
    C. refuse the map and pencil, but quickly give him a
       few basic directions which will lead him to the
       vicinity of his destination
    D. tell the driver to recheck the map carefully because
       it is easy to get to his destination

18. Suppose that, as a permanent bridge and tunnel officer,   18.___
    you have been temporarily assigned to train a newly ap-
    pointed officer. The new employee performed a certain
    task incorrectly in the past and you have explained the
    correct method to him. However, he has made the same
    error again.
    Of the following, the FIRST thing you should do is
    A. recommend that his poor performance be noted on
       his probationary report
    B. explain and demonstrate the correct method again
       and watch him perform the task for a while
    C. ignore the error unless the task is vitally impor-
       tant to the performance of his duties
    D. inform his supervisor of the new officer's inability
       to follow your directions

19. Assume that an officer has just collected a toll from a motorist and the car sideswipes another vehicle as they are proceeding onto the bridge. The two vehicles have stopped, partially blocking the approach to the bridge. Of the following, the FIRST thing the officer should do is
    A. issue a ticket to the driver who caused the accident
    B. write a detailed report of the accident
    C. leave his booth and administer first aid if it is needed
    D. stop all traffic in his lane and signal the other officers to do likewise

19.___

20. As a bridge and tunnel officer, you have just completed a tour of duty collecting tolls. While you are carrying the toll money, and officer in another toll booth calls to you: *My replacement has not shown up yet and I have an appointment to keep. What should I do?*
    Of the following, which *one* is the BEST response to make?
    A. *I'm not in a rush and I'd like to earn some over-time, so I'll replace you until he arrives.*
    B. *Call the supervisor and explain the whole situation to him.*
    C. *Close your toll booth now and leave a note explaining what happened.*
    D. *If you keep and eye on my toll money, I'll explain the situation to the supervisor.*

20.___

KEY (CORRECT ANSWERS)

1.	D	6.	D	11.	B	16.	B
2.	A	7.	A	12.	C	17.	C
3.	B	8.	B	13.	D	18.	B
4.	A	9.	C	14.	D	19.	D
5.	D	10.	C	15.	D	20.	B

TEST 2

DIRECTIONS: Each question or incomplete statement is followed by
several suggested answers or completions. Select the
one that BEST answers the question or completes the
statement. *PRINT THE LETTER OF THE CORRECT ANSWER IN
THE SPACE AT THE RIGHT.*

1.   Suppose that a car stops at a toll booth and a passenger   1.___
      in the rear of the car calls the officer in the booth a
      pig.
      Which *one* of the following would be the BEST action for the
      officer to take?
         A. Keep on guard for this person in the future, since
            he obviously represents a threat
         B. Tell the driver to pull over to his supervisor's
            post so that the supervisor can aid the officer in
            making a formal complaint
         C. Ignore the remark and continue performing his duties
         D. Issue a summons to the passenger because he insulted
            an officer

2.   Of the following situations, which one is LEAST likely   2.___
      to indicate possible danger inside a tunnel?
         A. A car has a flat tire and officers are directing
            traffic around it.
         B. The lights in the tunnel have suddenly dimmed.
         C. There is an accumulation of gasoline fumes, and it
            becomes difficult to breathe.
         D. There is a rise in temperature and smoke is visible
            in one portion of the tunnel.

3.   Officers should always be courteous to the people going   3.___
      by their toll booths MAINLY because
         A. courtesy helps them maintain good relations with
            the public
         B. courtesy allows them to enjoy their work more than
            if they always had to act formally
         C. someone might report an officer's bad manners
         D. courtesy will result in substantially higher reve-
            nues for the facility

4.   Suppose that, as a bridge and tunnel officer, you are at   4.___
      a post inside a tunnel. Your tour is almost over, but
      you feel feverish and weak.
      The BEST thing for you to do is to
         A. try to remain at your post, since your tour of duty
            is nearly ended
         B. walk to the next post in the tunnel and inform the
            officer there that you do not feel well
         C. take some aspirin, but contact someone of you feel
            drowsy
         D. contact your supervisor and tell him how you feel

Questions 5 - 10

DIRECTIONS: Answer Questions 5 through 10 SOLELY on the basis of
the information given in the chart below and the key
to abbreviations. The chart provides information about
the assignments of a group of Bridge and Tunnel Officers in City Y during the year.

Name of Officer	Date Assignment Made	Days Assigned	Tour of Duty	Facility	Station
Clark, Joseph	11/18	Tues.-Sat.	7 a.m- 3 p.m.	Seamans Tunnel	Post A
Feins, Arthur	10/22	Fri.-Tues.	11 p.m.- 7 a.m	Lyons Central Bridge	Lane 2
Fine, Howard	10/15	Mon.-Fri.	7 a.m.- 3 p.m.	Nimmons Street Bridge	Lane 2
Finia, Maria	11/25	Sat.-Wed.	3 p.m.- 11 p.m.	Nimmons Street Bridge	Lane 4
Rivera, Juan	11/25	Wed.-Sun.	3 p.m.- 11 p.m.	Seamans Tunnel	Post A
Sussman, Joan	10/15	Sun.-Thur.	11 p.m.- 7 a.m.	Livingston Tunnel	Post B
West, Michael	10/22	Fri.-Tues.	3 p.m.- 11 p.m.	Lyons Central Bridge	Lane 2

Key to abbreviations: Mon.- Monday   Fri.- Friday
                         Tues.- Tuesday   Sat.- Saturday
                         Wed.- Wednesday   Sun.- Sunday
                         Thur.- Thursday

5.   Which one of the following Officers had an assignment to   5.___
      the Nimmons Street Bridge dated 11/25?
          A. Joseph Clark   B. Howard Fine
          C. Maria Finia   D. Juan Rivera

6.   Which of the Officers was assigned to a Lane 2 station   6.___
      on October 15?
          A. Arthur Feins   B. Howard Fine
          C. Joan Sussman   D. Michael West

7. The Officers whose assignments were made AFTER
    November 19 are

    A. Juan Rivera and Michael West
    B. Maria Finia and Juan Rivera
    C. Joseph Clark, Maria Finia and Juan Rivera
    D. Arthur Feins, Howard Fine, Joan Sussman and
       Michael West

    7.____

8. The number of Officers assigned to work ONLY during
    p.m. hours is

    A. 2   B. 3   C. 4   D. 5

    8.____

9. How many Officers are NOT assigned to work on Sundays?

    A. 1   B. 2   C. 3   D. 4

    9.____

10. According to the above chart, two Officers were assigned
    to the same facility and station during the same days of
    the week, but they work different tours of duty.
    This station is NOT covered by either of these Officers
    on these days from

    A. 7 a.m. to 3 p.m.   B. 7 p.m. to 3 a.m.
    C. 3 p.m. to 11 p.m.   D. 11 p.m. to 7 a.m.

    10.____

Questions 11 - 18

DIRECTIONS: Answer Questions 11 through 18 ONLY on the basis of
               the Rules for Bridge and Tunnel Officers given below.

RULES FOR BRIDGE AND TUNNEL OFFICERS

I.   Officers shall give their name, rank, and badge number
     to any person who requests it.
II. An Officer on duty at a tunnel post shall immediately
     press the button for fire, obstructed lane, or dangerous
     vehicle when one of these conditions exists.
III. If the driver of a vehicle does not have the cash or
     stamped ticket to pay a toll, he shall not he allowed
     to use the facility.
IV. An Officer shall permit only authorized persons on of-
     ficial business to be in a toll booth or at a tunnel
     post.
V.   An Officer in a toll booth shall get assistance from
     his supervisor in any situation when he is unsure
     whether a vehicle should be allowed to proceed.

11. An Officer collects the correct toll from a truck driver.   11.___
    However, the driver says that bridge tolls are too high
    and in an angry voice asks the Officer for his name and
    number so that he can write a letter about the high tolls.
    Of the following, the BEST thing for the Officer to do is
    to
    A. tell the driver that he is holding up traffic and
       should move on
    B. give his name and badge number to the driver
    C. tell the driver not to use the bridge anymore if
       the toll is too high
    D. provide the driver with reasons for the tolls
       charged

12. While on duty at a post in a tunnel, an Officer notices   12.___
    a driver putting out a small fire in the engine of a car.
    At that moment, the driver turns to the Officer and yells
    I can put it out myself.
    The FIRST thing the Officer should do is
    A. help the driver put out the fire
    B. press the button which signals a fire in the tunnel
    C. let the motorist handle the situation himself
    D. call his supervisor and ask for help

13. A motorist approaching a bridge stops at a toll booth   13.___
    and hands the Officer postage stamps, instead of coins
    to pay the toll.
    The Officer should FIRST
    A. *refuse* the stamps and tell the driver that the
       bridge toll must be paid in cash
    B. *accept* the stamps as payment of the toll
    C. *request* assistance in dealing with the situation
    D. *refuse* the stamps, let the vehicle go on, but have
       the driver promise that he will return with the
       money

14. An Officer at a post inside a tunnel sees two large   14.___
    cartons fall off a truck.
    The Officer's FIRST response should be to
    A. try to move the cartons to the side of the roadway
    B. signal another Officer to stop the truck at the
       tunnel's exit
    C. run after the truck to tell the driver what has
       happened
    D. use an appropriate signal button

15. Suppose that, while an Officer is collecting tolls, a
    car stops at the toll booth and the driver appears to
    be drunk.
    Of the following, the First thing the Officer should do
    is to
    A. tell the driver to proceed very carefully and be
       sure not to drive after drinking in the future
    B. signal another Officer to assist him in escorting
       the driver to their supervisor
    C. refuse to accept the toll money and call his super-
       visor
    D. immediately press the emergency button

15.___

16. While on duty inside a tunnel, an Officer notices that
    a car has stopped and has a flat tire. It is late eve-
    ning and there is no other traffic visible.
    The FIRST thing the Officer should do is to
    A. quickly assist the driver in changing the tire
    B. signal that a lane is blocked
    C. tell the driver to drive out of the tunnel
    D. issue a summons to the motorist for stopping his
       car inside the tunnel

16.___

17. Suppose that a friend tells an Officer that he is inter-
    ested in learning about the Officer's work. The friend
    says that he would like to visit the Officer in a toll
    booth for an hour the next day.
    Of the following, which *one* is the BEST reply for the
    Officer to make?
    A. *Sorry, but I'm not allowed to let you in the booth.*
    B. *You can stay in the booth, but be careful not to
       touch anything.*
    C. *You can't come inside the booth, but you can stay
       with me in the tunnel.*
    D. *It's all right, but be sure to give my name, rank
       and number if anyone questions you.*

17.___

18. Assume that, while an Officer is collecting a toll from
    a motorist, the Officer sees a child tied up in the rear
    of the car.
    Of the following, the BEST thing for the Officer to do is
    to
    A. ignore what he has seen and continue collecting tolls
    B. try to delay the car, and signal for assistance
    C. reach into the car and untie the child
    D. tell the driver that he cannot use the bridge unless
       he unties the child

18.___

19. Assume that an officer reported the following amounts   19.___
    of toll monies collected during each day of a five-day
    period:

Tuesday	$324.75
Wednesday	$299.25
Thursday	$391.75
Friday	$486.25
Saturday	$167.50

    The *total amount* of toll money collected during this
    period was
    A. $1570.25   B. $1648.50   C. $1669.50   D. $1699.75

20. Suppose that during a two-hour period in a toll booth   20.___
    an officer collected the following:

Type of Money	Number of Bills
$20 bills	2
$10 bills	5
$ 5 bills	23
$ 1 bills	269

    The *total amount* of money the officer collected was
    A. $299   B. $464   C. $474   D. $501

KEY (CORRECT ANSWERS)

1.	C	6.	B	11.	B	16.	B
2.	A	7.	B	12.	B	17.	A
3.	A	8.	B	13.	A	18.	B
4.	D	9.	B	14.	D	19.	C
5.	C	10.	A	15.	C	20.	C

EXAMINATION SECTION

TEST 1

DIRECTIONS: Each question or incomplete statement is followed by several suggested answers or completions. Select the one that BEST answers the question or completes the statement. *PRINT THE LETTER OF THE CORRECT ANSWER IN THE SPACE AT THE RIGHT.*

Questions 1-8.

DIRECTIONS: Answer Questions 1 through 8 SOLELY on the basis of the diagram and instructions given below and on the following page.

Assume that the diagram below represents vehicles waiting in five toll lanes, numbered 1 through 5. Each vehicle is also labelled with a different capital letter. The symbols used for each type of vehicle are as follows:

motorcycle   car   car with trailer   bus   truck

Each symbol for a truck also includes a symbol for each axle of the truck.
The symbol for an axle is [   ]

A three-axle truck, therefore, is represented by the following symbol:

DIAGRAM OF VEHICLES WAITING IN TOLL LANES

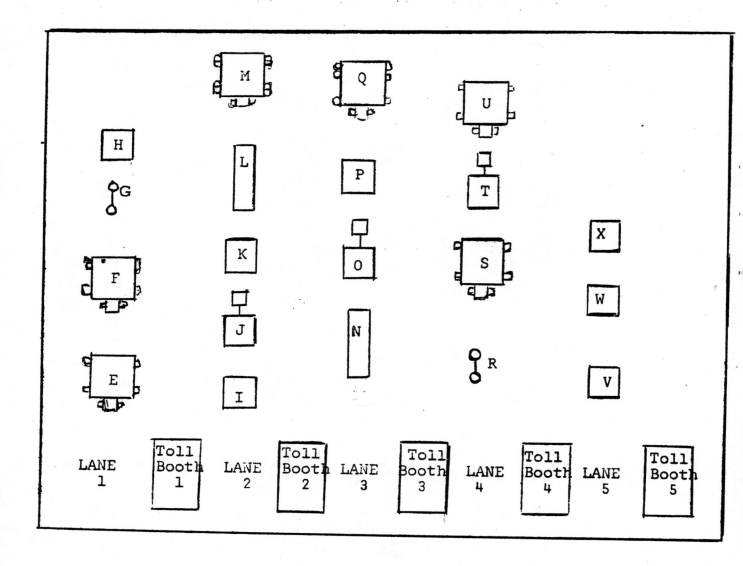

SAMPLE QUESTION

The third vehicle from the toll booth in Lane 3 is a
A. four-axle truck   B. car with trailer
C. car   D. bus

Counting from the beginning of Lane 3 at the bottom of the
diagram, the third vehicle is labelled P. The shape of the symbol
for vehicle P is the same shape as the symbol for a car.
Therefore, the CORRECT answer is C.

1. Which lane contains ONLY a single type of vehicle?   1.___
    A. 1   B. 3   C. 4   D. 5

2. Which lanes contain AT LEAST one motorcycle?   2.___
    A. 1 and 4   B. 1, 2, and 4
    C. 3 and 4   D. 3, 4, and 5

3. A car is in front of a bus in lane
   A. 1   B. 2   C. 3   D. 4

   3.___

4. Which one of the following types of vehicles is NOT waiting in Lane 2?
   A. Motorcycle   B. Bus
   C. Car with trailer   D. Truck

   4.___

5. Which vehicle is a four-axle truck?
   A. E   B. F   C. Q   D. U

   5.___

6. Which lane contains MORE than one three-axle truck?
   A. 1   B. 2   C. 3   D. 4

   6.___

7. Which one of the following vehicles is in line with a car *directly in front of* it and a car *directly behind* it?
   A. J   B. Q   C. T   D. X

   7.___

8. Which one of the following types of vehicles is NOT waiting in EITHER Lane 3 or Lane 4?
   A. Car   B. Four-axle truck
   C. Five-axle truck   D. Bus

   8.___

9. Suppose that an officer carried two packages, one weighing 73 pounds and the other weighing 41 pounds 3 ounces. The DIFFERENCE between the weights of the two packages was ____ pounds ____ ounces.
   A. 31; 5   B. 31; 13   C. 32; 6   D. 32; 12

   9.___

10. Suppose that the toll money collected at a bridge during March of last year was $153,696.
If the toll money collected at this bridge in April was 3% higher than in March, then the April total was MOST NEARLY
   A. $149,085   B. $158,307   C. $167,431   D. $200,075

   10.___

11. Suppose that 10% more vehicles crossed a certain bridge on Friday than on the previous day.
If 18,100 cars, 1,290 trucks, and 130 buses used the bridge on Thursday, how many cars, trucks, and buses crossed the bridge on Friday?
   A. 17,568   B. 18,144   C. 19,520   D. 21,472

   11.___

12. The maximum height allowed for vehicles using a particular bridge under normal conditions is 13 feet 6 inches. If a vehicle is 15 feet 5 inches tall, by exactly what amount does the vehicle EXCEED the maximum height limit for this bridge? ____ foot(feet) ____ inch(es).
   A. 1; 9   B. 1; 11   C. 2; 1   D. 2; 3

   12.___

13. The number of cars, trucks, and buses using two different toll lanes on a certain day was as follows:

	Lane 1	Lane 2
Cars	994	1086
Trucks	113	51
Buses	31	16

   13.___

A comparison of these two lanes would show that the TOTAL number of cars, trucks, and buses using Lane 1 on that day was ____ than the total at Lane 2.
    A. 15 less   B. 25 less   C. 15 more   D. 25 more

14. A certain officer was assigned to collect tolls for two hours. The officer was given $80 in various bills and $150 in quarters so that he could make change. He placed this money in a drawer in the toll booth. At the end of the two hours of toll collecting, the officer had a total of $1,375.75 in the drawer.
The percent of this total which represents the tolls collected is MOST NEARLY
    A. 15%   B. 63%   C. 78%   D. 83%

14. ___

Questions 15-20.

DIRECTIONS: Answer Questions 15 through 20 SOLELY on the basis of the chart and the instructions given below.

Toll Rate	$.25	$.30	$.45	$.60	$.75	$.90	$1.20	$2.50
Classification Number of Vehicle	1	2	3	4	5	6	7	8

Assume that each of the amounts of money on the above chart is a toll rate charged for a type of vehicle and that the nummber immediately below each amount is the classification number for that type of vehicle. For instance, "1" is the classification number for a vehicle paying a $.25 toll; "2" is the classification number for a vehicle paying a $.30 toll; and so forth.

In each question, a series of tolls is given in Column I. Column II gives four different arrangements of classification numbers. You are to pick the answer (A, B, C, or D) in Column II that gives the classification numbers that match the tolls in Column I and are in the same order as the tolls in Column I.

SAMPLE QUESTION:

Column I

$.30, $.90, $2.50, $.45

Column II

A. 2, 6, 8, 2
B. 2, 8, 6, 3
C. 2, 6, 8, 3
D. 1, 6, 8, 3

According to the chart, the classification numbers that correspond to these toll rates are as follows: $.30 - 2, $.90 - 6, $2.50 - 8, $.45 - 3. Therefore, the CORRECT answer is 2, 6, 8, 3. This answer is C in Column II. Do the following questions in the same way.

Column I	Column II	
15. $.60, $.30, $.90, $1.20, $.60	A. 4, 6, 2, 8, 4 B. 4, 2, 6, 7, 4 C. 2, 4, 7, 6, 2 D. 2, 4, 6, 7, 4	15.___
16. $.90, $.45, $.25, $.45, $2.50, $.75	A. 6, 3, 1, 3, 8, 3 B. 6, 3, 3, 1, 8, 5 C. 6, 1, 3, 3, 8, 5 D. 6, 3, 1, 3, 8, 5	16.___
17. $.45, $.75, $1.20, $.25 $.25, $.30, $.45	A. 3, 5, 7, 1, 1, 2, 3 B. 5, 3, 7, 1, 1, 2, 3 C. 3, 5, 7, 1, 2, 1, 3 D. 3, 7, 5, 1, 1, 2, 3	17.___
18. $1.20, $2.50, $.45, $.90, $1.20, $.75, $.25	A. 7, 8, 5, 6, 7, 5, 1 B. 7, 8, 3, 7, 6, 5, 1 C. 7, 8, 3, 6, 7, 5, 1 D. 7, 8, 3, 6, 7, 1, 5	18.___
19. $2.50, $1.20, $.90, $.25, $.60, $.45, $.30	A. 8, 6, 7, 1, 4, 3, 2 B. 8, 7, 5, 1, 4, 3, 2 C. 8, 7, 6, 2, 4, 3, 2 D. 8, 7, 6, 1, 4, 3, 2	19.___
20. $.75, $.25, $.45, $.60, $.90, $.30, $2.50	A. 5, 1, 3, 2, 4, 6, 8 B. 5, 1, 3, 4, 2, 6, 8 C. 5, 1, 3, 4, 6, 2, 8 D. 5, 3, 1, 4, 6, 2, 8	20.___

KEY (CORRECT ANSWERS)

1. D		11. D	
2. A		12. B	
3. B		13. A	
4. A		14. D	
5. C		15. B	
6. D		16. D	
7. A		17. A	
8. C		18. C	
9. B		19. D	
10. B		20. C	

TEST 2

DIRECTIONS: Each question or incomplete statement is followed by several suggested answers or completions. Select the one that BEST answers the question or completes the statement. *PRINT THE LETTER OF THE CORRECT ANSWER IN THE SPACE AT THE RIGHT.*

Questions 1-10.

DIRECTIONS: Answer Questions 1 through 10 SOLELY on the basis of the information given in the following chart which shows the toll rates charged for various types of vehicles using the bridges and tunnels in Grand City.

TOLL RATES FOR BRIDGES AND TUNNELS IN GRAND CITY

Vehicle Type	Main Street Bridge	Wilson Tunnel	Memorial Bridge	Fillmore Bridge	Jackson Avenue Tunnel
Two-axle vehicle weighing less than 8000 pounds, including cars, trucks, and buses	$ .50	$ .75	$ .25	$ .60	$ .75
Passenger automobile with trailer	$ .75	$1.00	$ .50	$ .90	$1.00
Two-axle vehicle weighing more than 8000 pounds	$1.00	$1.25	$ .80	$1.30	$1.40
Three-axle vehicle	$1.25	$1.50	$1.10	$1.75	$1.80
Four-axle vehicle	$1.75	$1.80	$1.40	$2.00	$2.30
Each additional axle	$ .50	$ .40	$ .40	$ .50	$ .50

1. According to the above chart, the HIGHEST toll charged
.for a three-axle vehicle using a bridge is
   A. $1.40   B. $1.75   C. $1.80   D. $2.30

   1.___

2. The TOTAL amount of money paid in tolls for a passenger
car with a trailer going through the Wilson Tunnel and
across the Fillmore Bridge is
   A. $1.35   B. $1.50   C. $1.90   D. $2.00

   2.___

3. Of the following, the LOWEST toll charged for a two-axle truck weighing 6000 pounds is at the
   A. Main Street Bridge   B. Wilson Tunnel
   C. Jackson Avenue Tunnel   D. Fillmore Bridge

3._____

4. The toll charged for driving a five-axle vehicle through the Wilson Tunnel is
   A. $1.80   B. $2.20   C. $2.30   D. $2.80

4._____

5. Of the following, the type of vehicle for which the LEAST amount in tolls is charged on each of the three bridges is a
   A. passenger car with a trailer
   B. two-axle truck weighing 8,200 pounds
   C. three-axle truck
   D. four-axle truck

5._____

6. The DIFFERENCE between the tolls charged for a three-axle vehicle using the Memorial Bridge and a three-axle vehicle using the Jackson Avenue Tunnel is
   A. $.40   B. $.50   C. $.60   D. $.70

6._____

7. The DIFFERENCE between the tolls charged for a four-axle vehicle using the Wilson Tunnel and a three-axle vehicle using the same tunnel is
   A. $.25   B. $.30   C. $.40   D. $.50

7._____

8. The TOTAL amount charged for tolls for a five-axle truck going through the Jackson Avenue Tunnel and across the Memorial Bridge is
   A. $3.70   B. $4.10   C. $4.30   D. $4.60

8._____

9. According to the above chart, which of the following vehicles would be charged the HIGHEST toll?
   A
   A. passenger car with trailer using the Fillmore Bridge
   B. three-axle truck using the Wilson Tunnel
   C. three-axle truck using the Jackson Avenue Tunnel
   D. four-axle truck using the Main Street Bridge

9._____

10. A three-axle truck using the Fillmore Bridge is charged the SAME toll as a
    A. 4000-pound car using the Jackson Avenue Tunnel
    B. three-axle truck using the Main Street Bridge
    C. four-axle truck using the Main Street Bridge
    D. five-axle truck using the Memorial Bridge

10._____

11. The number of vehicles using a particular lane each hour during a 6-hour period varied as follows: 134, 210, 213, 234, 111, 118.
    The AVERAGE number of vehicles per hour using the toll lane during this period was
    A. 150   B. 160   C. 170   D. 180

11._____

12. Assume that, as a bridge and tunnel officer, you have   12.____
    been assigned to a shift which begins at 2:00 P.M., and
    you want to arrive 10 minutes before the shift begins.
    If you average 28 miles per hour while driving to work
    and must travel 21 miles, at exactly what time should you
    START driving to work? ____ P.M.
         A. 12:30   B. 12:40   C. 1:05   D. 1:15

Questions 13-16.

DIRECTIONS: Questions 13 through 16 are based on the Instructions,
              the Bridge and Tunnel Officer's Toll Report form, and
              the Situation given below. The questions ask how the
              report form should be filled in based on the Instructions
              and the information given in the Situation.

INSTRUCTIONS

Assume that a Bridge and Tunnel Officer on duty in a toll booth
must make an entry on the following report form immediately after
each incident in which a vehicle driver does not pay the correct toll.

```
+---------------------------------------------------------------------+
|        BRIDGE AND TUNNEL OFFICER'S TOLL REPORT                      |
|                                                                     |
|   Officer _____    Date _____  |
|                                                                     |
|            Type of      Toll                                        |
|     Time   Vehicle    Collected     Explanation of Entry            |
|                                                                     |
|  1. ____   _____     _____      _____   |
|                                                                     |
|  2. ____   _____     _____      _____   |
|                                                                     |
|     ____   _____     _____      _____   |
+---------------------------------------------------------------------+
```

SITUATION

John McDonald is a Bridge and Tunnel Officer assigned to toll
booth 4, between the hours of 11 P.M. and 1 A.M. On this particular
tour, two incidents occurred. At 11:43 P.M., a five-axle truck
stopped at the toll booth and Officer McDonald collected a $.75 toll
from the driver. As the truck passed, he realized the toll should
have been $1.25, and he quickly copied the vehicle's license plate
number as M724HJ. At 12:34 A.M., a motorcycle went through toll
lane 4 without paying the toll. The motorcycle did not have any
license plate.

13. The entry which should be made on line 1 in the second   13.____
    column is
         A. 11:43 P.M.   B. 12:34 A.M.
         C. five-axle truck   D. motorcycle

14. The above passage does NOT provide the information   14.___
    necessary to fill in which of the following items?
    A. Officer   B. Date
    C. Line 1, Toll Collected   D. Line 2, Time

15. Of the following, the BEST place to fill in the statement   15.___
    Non-payment of toll -- no license plate on vehicle is on
    line
    A. 1, Type of Vehicle   B. 1, Explanation of Entry
    C. 2, Type of Vehicle   D. 2, Explanation of Entry

16. What should Officer McDonald have written for *Toll*   16.___
    Collected on line 1?
    A. $.75   B. $1.25
    C. $11.43   D. No toll collected

Questions 17-20.

DIRECTIONS: Answer Questions 17 through 20 SOLELY on the basis of
              the information given in the passage below.

*A summons is an official statement ordering a person to appear
in court.   In traffic violation situations, summonses are used when
arrests need not be made.   The main reason for traffic summonses is
to deter motorists from repeating the same traffic violation.
Occasionally, motorists may make unintentional driving errors, and
sometimes they are unaware of correct driving regulations.   In cases
such as these, the policy should be to have the Officer verbally
inform the motorist of the violation and warn him against repeating
it.   The purpose of this practice is not to limit the number of
summonses, but rather to prevent the issuing of summonses when the
violation is not due to deliberate intent or to inexcusable negligence.*

17. According to the above passage, the PRINCIPAL reason for   17.___
    issuing traffic summonses is to
    A. discourage motorists from violating these laws again
    B. increase the money collected by the city
    C. put traffic violators in prison
    D. have them serve as substitutes for police officers

18. The reason a verbal warning may sometimes be substituted   18.___
    for a summons is to
    A. limit the number of summonses
    B. distinguish between excusable and inexcusable
       violations
    C. provide harsher penalties for deliberate intent than
       for inexcusable negligence
    D. decrease the caseload in the courts

19. The above passage implies that someone who violated a   19.___
    traffic regulation because he did NOT know about the
    regulation should be
    A. put under arrest   B. fined less money
    C. given a summons   D. told not to do it again

20. Using the distinctions made by the above passage, the one 20.___
    of the following motorists to whom it would be MOST
    desirable to issue a summons is the one who exceeded the
    speed limit because he
      A. did not know the speed limit
      B. was late for an important business appointment
      C. speeded to avoid being hit by another car
      D. had a speedometer which was not working properly

―――

KEY (CORRECT ANSWERS)

1.	B	11.	C
2.	C	12.	C
3.	A	13.	C
4.	B	14.	B
5.	A	15.	D
6.	D	16.	A
7.	B	17.	A
8.	D	18.	B
9.	C	19.	D
10.	C	20.	B

―――

EXAMINATION SECTION

TEST 1

DIRECTIONS: Each question or incomplete statement is followed by several suggested answers or completions. Select the one that BEST answers the question or completes the statement. *PRINT THE LETTER OF THE CORRECT ANSWER IN THE SPACE AT THE RIGHT.*

Questions 1-8.

DIRECTIONS: Questions 1 through 8 are to be answered SOLELY on the basis of the following information and relief schedule. Read the information and look at the relief schedule before you begin answering these questions.

The daily activities of individual Bridge and Tunnel Officers are listed on their relief schedule. Below is the relief schedule of Officer Franklin Pierce for March 20.

OFFICER: Pierce		
TIME	**RELIEF SCHEDULE**	**LANES**
6:55 A.M. - 7:15 A.M.	Relieves Officer Rodgers	6
7:20 A.M. - 7:50 A.M.	Relieves Officer Smith	7
7:55 A.M. - 8:15 A.M.	Officer Pierce takes his own relief	
8:20 A.M. - 8:40 A.M.	Relieves Officer Jones	4
8:45 A.M. - 9:15 A.M.	Relieves Officer Thomas	5
9:20 A.M. - 10:10 A.M.	Officer Pierce has tow truck duty	
10:15 A.M. - 11:05 A.M.	Officer Pierce takes his own meal	
11:10 A.M. - 12 Noon	Relieves Officer Rodgers for a meal	6
12:05 P.M. - 12:35 P.M.	Relieves Officer James	2
12:40 P.M. - 1:30 P.M.	Relieves Officer Jones for a meal	4
1:35 P.M. - 2:05 P.M.	Officer Pierce takes his own relief	
2:10 P.M. - 3:00 P.M.	Relieves Officer Peterson for a meal	3
3:05 P.M. - 3:55 P.M.	Officer Pierce assists the Sergeant	
4:20 P.M.	Officer Pierce terminates tour of duty	

1. During which one of the following time periods is Officer Pierce scheduled for tow truck duty?
    A. 7:55 AM - 8:15 AM
    B. 9:20 AM - 10:10 AM
    C. 10:15 AM - 11:05 AM
    D. 1:35 PM - 2:05 PM

    1.____

2. At 12:15 P.M., Officer Pierce should be working in lane number
    A. 2
    B. 3
    C. 4
    D. 6

    2.____

3. How many times does Officer Pierce relieve other officers
   for a meal?   3.___
   A. 1   B. 2   C. 3   D. 4

4. Officer Jones' meal period begins at 12:40 P.M.   4.___
   At what time does his meal period end?
   _____ P.M.
   A. 1:30   B. 1:35   C. 1:40   D. 2:05

5. At what time is Officer Pierce scheduled for his own meal?   5.___
   A. 9:20 AM - 10:10 AM   B. 10:15 AM - 11:05 AM
   C. 11:10 AM - 12 Noon   D. 1:35 PM - 2:05 PM

6. Officer Rodgers is relieved by Officer Pierce for a meal.   6.___
   How long is Officer Rodgers' meal period?
   _____ minutes.
   A. 20   B. 30   C. 45   D. 50

7. The assignment which Officer Pierce is scheduled to   7.___
   perform immediately before his own meal time is
   A. tow truck duty
   B. relieving Officer Thomas
   C. assisting the Sergeant
   D. relieving Officer Rodgers for a meal

8. At what time does Officer Pierce's tour of duty end for   8.___
   March 20?
   _____ P.M.
   A. 2:05   B. 3:00   C. 3:55   D. 4:20

Questions 9-15.

DIRECTIONS: Questions 9 through 15 are to be answered SOLELY on the
              basis of the information and the CLASSIFICATION NUMBER
              CHART shown below and on the following page.

The Bridge and Tunnel Authority charges tolls on vehicles using
its facilities according to vehicle type, axle count, and weight. To
standardize the tolls to be charged, a Classification Number System
has been established which is based upon the various possible com-
binations of vehicle type, number of axles, and weights.

CLASSIFICATION NUMBER CHART

Classification Number	Type of Vehicle	Number of Axles	Weight
2	Cars, Mobile Homes	2	Various
2	Motorcycles	2	Various
2	Ambulances	2	Various
2	Vehicles weighing 6,000 lbs. & under	2	Various
3	Passenger car with one-axle trailer	3	Various
4	Truck	2	Over 7,000 lbs.
5	Truck	3	Over 12,000 lbs, but under 16,000 lbs.
6	Trailer Truck	4	No weight limit
7	Tank Truck	5	Over 17,000 lbs.

9. The CORRECT Classification Number for a two-axle mobile home weighing over 7,000 lbs. is
   A. 2   B. 3   C. 4   D. 5

9.____

10. The CORRECT Classification Number for a two-axle vehicle weighing 5,500 lbs. is
    A. 2   B. 4   C. 5   D. 7

10.____

11. The CORRECT Classification Number for a tank truck with five axles and weighing 18,000 lbs. is
    A. 3   B. 4   C. 5   D. 7

11.____

12. For a truck weighing 11,000 lbs. to be CORRECTLY classified as Classification Number 4, the number of axles it must have is
    A. 2   B. 3   C. 4   D. 5

12.____

13. A passenger car towing a one-axle trailer weighing 250 lbs. is CORRECTLY classified as Classification Number
    A. 2   B. 3   C. 4   D. 5

13.____

14. For a tank truck to be properly classified as Classification Number 7, it must weigh _____ than _____ lbs. and have _____ axles.
    A. less; 7,000; two   B. more; 12,000; three
    C. less; 16,000; four   D. more; 17,000; five

14.____

15. The one of the following vehicles which is NOT correctly classified as Classification Number 2 is a(n)
    A. ambulance
    B. motorcycle
    C. trailer truck
    D. passenger car weighing 5,100 lbs.

15.____

Questions 16-22.

DIRECTIONS: Questions 16 through 22 are to be answered SOLELY on
the basis of the Bridge and Tunnel Toll Rate Chart below

BRIDGE AND TUNNEL TOLL RATES

Type of Vehicle	Axles	Weight	Toll
Passenger Car	2	All weights	$1.25
Mobile Home	3	Over 7,000 lbs.	.75
Motorcycle	2	All weights	.85
Truck	2	Over 7,000 lbs.	1.75
Truck	2	Under 7,000 lbs.	1.40
Passenger Car with 2-axle Trailer	4	All weights	1.95
Flatbed Truck	3	Over 25,000 lbs.	2.55
Trailer Truck	4	Under 25,000 lbs.	3.20
Tank Truck	5	Over 22,000 lbs.	4.25
Private Bus	2	Over 15,000 lbs.	1.15
Private Bus	3	Over 18,000 lbs.	2.00
Public Bus	2	All weights	Free
Police and Fire Department Vehicles	Unlimited	All weights	Free

16. A driver in a passenger car pulling a two-axle trailer should pay a toll of
A. $.75   B. $.85   C. $1.25   D. $1.95

17. The HIGHEST toll that can be charged on a vehicle with four axles and weighing 24,500 lbs. is
A. $1.95   B. $2.55   C. $3.20   D. $4.25

18. A driver of a two-axle truck weighing 6,100 lbs. should be charged a toll of
A. $.75   B. $1.40   C. $1.75   D. $3.20

19. A mobile home has three axles and weighs 11,200 lbs. This vehicle should pay a toll of
A. $.75   B. $.85   C. $1.15   D. $2.00

20. Bridge and Tunnel Officer Edwards has 3 buses coming to his toll booth: a private bus weighing 25,000 lbs. with 3 axles, a public bus weighing 22,000 lbs. with 2 axles, and a private bus weighing 16,000 lbs. with 2 axles. The TOTAL amount Officer Edwards should collect for these three buses is
A. $3.15   B. $4.00   C. $4.30   D. $5.15

21. A passenger car driven by Alvin Charles weighs 5,940 lbs. Mr. Charles should pay a toll of
A. $.75   B. $.85   C. $1.25   D. $1.75

22. A three-axle flatbed truck weighing 28,000 lbs. should pay   22.____
    a toll of
        A. $2.00   B. $2.55   C. $3.20   D. $4.25

Questions 23-27.

DIRECTIONS: Questions 23 through 27 are to be answered on the basis
              of the following information.

      The Classon City Bridge and Tunnel Authority requires that all
officers collect tolls when on duty. Toll collection is an
important part of the job, and all transactions should be accurate.

23. A car with a trailer attached to it arrives at the toll   23.____
    booth of Officer Anderson. Officer Anderson tells the
    driver that the toll for this vehicle and trailer is
    $1.40. The driver hands Officer Anderson a $5.00 bill.
    How much change should Officer Anderson return to the
    driver?
        A. $3.40   B. $3.50   C. $3.60   D. $3.70

24. Mr. Eric Knoll arrives at the toll booth of Officer Piton.   24.____
    The correct toll for his vehicle is $3.85. Knoll mis-
    takenly gives Officer Piton $2.55.
    Officer Piton should collect an additional
        A. $1.15   B. $1.30   C. $1.35   D. $1.65

25. A truck driver comes into the lane of Officer Enid. The   25.____
    toll for his vehicle is $2.85. He informs Officer Enid
    that he also wants to pay for the truck immediately
    behind his. The toll for the second truck is also $2.85.
    If the truck driver paid for both vehicles, the CORRECT
    change from a $20.00 bill would be
        A. $14.30   B. $14.45   C. $14.60   D. $15.30

26. A funeral procession of 8 cars approaches Officer Bragg's   26.____
    lane. The driver of the lead car asks Officer Bragg to
    charge him for all 8 cars. The toll for each individual
    car is $.75.
    How much change should Officer Bragg return after
    receiving a $10.00 bill?
        A. $2.00   B. $3.80   C. $4.00   D. $4.50

27. A truck driver approaches Officer Kendall's lane. The   27.____
    toll for the truck is $7.20. After the driver hands
    Officer Kendall a $10.00 bill, he drives away, forget-
    ting his change.
    How much change should the driver have received?
        A. $1.80   B. $2.20   C. $2.60   D. $2.80

Questions 28-32.

DIRECTIONS: Questions 28 through 32 are to be answered SOLELY on the
              basis of the following map and the following information

        Toll collectors answer motorists' questions concerning directions
by reading a map of the metropolitan area.   Although many alternate
routes leading to destinations exist on the following map, you are to
choose the MOST direct route of those given.

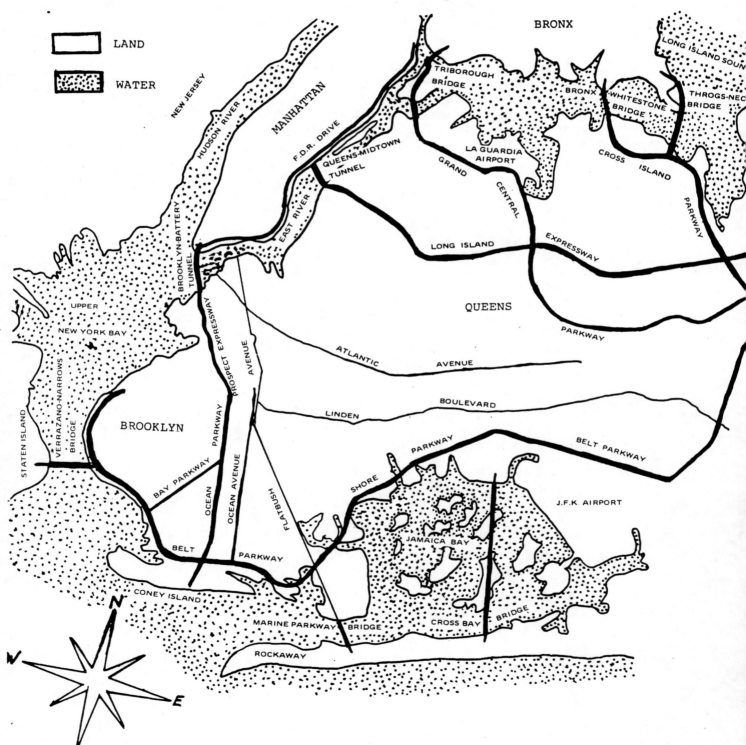

28. A motorist driving from the Bronx over the Triborough
    Bridge wants to go to La Guardia Airport in Queens.
    The officer should direct him to
       A. Grand Central Parkway   B. F.D.R. Drive
       C. Shore Parkway   D. Flatbush Avenue

28.___

29. A motorist driving from Manhattan through the Queens
    Midtown Tunnel would travel DIRECTLY onto
       A. Shore Parkway   B. F.D.R. Drive
       C. Long Island Expressway   D. Atlantic Avenue

29.___

30. A motorist traveling north over the Marine Parkway Bridge
    should take which route to reach Coney Island?
       A. Shore Parkway East   B. Belt Parkway West
       C. Linden Boulevard   D. Ocean Parkway

30.___

31. Which facility does NOT connect the Bronx and Queens?
       A. Triborough Bridge   B. Bronx-Whitestone Bridge
       C. Verrazano-Narrows Bridge D. Throgs-Neck Bridge

31.___

32. A motorist driving from Manhattan arrives at the toll
    booth of the Brooklyn-Battery Tunnel and asks directions
    to Ocean Parkway.
    To which one of the following routes should the motorist
    FIRST be directed?
       A. Atlantic Avenue   B. Bay Parkway
       C. Prospect Expressway   D. Ocean Avenue

32.___

Questions 33-40.

DIRECTIONS: Questions 33 through 40 are to be answered SOLELY on
              the basis of the following information concerning the
              limitations the Bridge and Tunnel Authority has placed
              on vehicles using its various facilities. The limita-
              tions list the names of potentially dangerous materials
              that may or may not be carried by these vehicles and
              specify the maximum height, weight, and width of
              vehicles allowed to use each facility.

MATERIALS LIST

PROHIBITED	PERMITTED
Dynamite	Battery Fluid
Gasoline	Cotton
Mercury	Helium
Propane	Rubber

VEHICLE LIMITATIONS

Maximum Width Permitted on All Bridges: 8 feet 6 inches
Maximum Width Permitted on All Tunnels: 7 feet

Maximum Height of Vehicle Permitted on Bridges and in Tunnels:

York Bridge	11 feet 2 inches
Bay Bridge	12 feet 10 inches
Bond Bridge	10 feet 2 inches
Old Town Bridge	15 feet 2 inches
Canal Bridge	14 feet 8 inches
Ribbon Bridge	14 feet 6 inches
State Bridge	13 feet
Borough Tunnel	12 feet
Ocean Tunnel	11 feet 10 inches

Maximum Weight Permitted on All Bridges and Tunnels: 22,000 lbs.

33. Which one of the following facilities allows a vehicle   33.__
    with a height of 15 feet?
    A. Bay Bridge   B. Ribbon Bridge
    C. Old Town Bridge   D. Canal Bridge

34. The MAXIMUM height of a vehicle allowed to use the Bond   34.__
    Bridge is _____ feet _____ inches.
        A. 10; 2   B. 11; 10   C. 14; 6   D, 14; 8

35. A vehicle with a height of 13 feet is permitted passage   35.__
    on which one of the following facilities?
    _____ Bridge.
        A. York   B. Canal   C. Bay   D. Bond

36. A truck weighing 18,000 lbs., 8 feet wide, with a height   36.__
    of 11 feet, and carrying helium is permitted in or on
    which one of the following?
        A. Borough Tunnel   B. Ocean Tunnel
        C. York Bridge   D. Bond Bridge

37. A flatbed trailer 7 feet 2 inches in width and 14 feet   37.__
    7 inches in height is permitted passage in or on which
    one of the following facilities?
        A. Canal Bridge   B. Ocean Tunnel
        C. Borough Tunnel   D. Ribbon Bridge

38. When Paul Smith arrives at Toll Booth I of the Borough   38.__
    Tunnel, he is told by the officer on duty that because
    of the tank truck's contents, he may not drive through
    the tunnel.
    For Mr. Smith's truck to be barred from the tunnel, he
    must be carrying
        A. battery fluid   B. propane
        C. helium   D. rubber

39. Officer Ellen Maye refuses passage to a flatbed truck trying to cross the Bay Bridge. The truck is carrying a crane, and the total height of the truck and crane is 14 feet.
This load exceeds the Bay Bridge's maximum height limit by exactly _____ foot _____ inches.
   A. 1; 0   B. 1; 2   C. 1; 3   D. 1; 5

     39. ___

40. A truck weighing 20,000 lbs., 8 feet 5 inches wide, and 11 feet high, and carrying cotton should be directed to use the Bay Bridge rather than the Borough Tunnel because of the truck's
   A. height   B. contents   C. weight   D. width

     40. ___

KEY (CORRECT ANSWERS)

1. B	11. D	21. C	31. C
2. A	12. A	22. B	32. C
3. C	13. B	23. C	33. C
4. A	14. D	24. B	34. A
5. B	15. C	25. A	35. B
6. D	16. D	26. C	36. C
7. A	17. C	27. D	37. A
8. D	18. B	28. A	38. B
9. A	19. A	29. C	39. B
10. A	20. A	30. B/D	40. D

TEST 2

DIRECTIONS: Each question or incomplete statement is followed by several suggested answers or completions. Select the one that BEST answers the question or completes the statement. *PRINT THE LETTER OF THE CORRECT ANSWER IN THE SPACE AT THE RIGHT.*

1. How much change should a motorist receive from a $20.00   1.___
   bill if his toll for using a tunnel is $2.65?
     A. $16.35   B. $16.65   C. $17.25   D. $17.35

2. On certain days, there are motorists who fail to pay the   2.___
   appropriate toll. On one day, this occurred four times.
   The unpaid tolls consisted of one for $2.15, two for
   $3.70 each, and another for $4.10.
   The TOTAL amount of tolls not paid was
     A. $9.95   B. $13.15   C. $13.65   D. $13.85

Questions 3-10.

DIRECTIONS: Questions 3 through 10 are to be answered SOLELY on the basis of the following information.

The Lawrence City Bridge and Tunnel Authority has rules about specific vehicles crossing its facilities. Oversize, or wide-load, overheight, and overweight vehicles, as well as vehicles carrying dangerous materials, may not be allowed on certain facilities.

LAWRENCE CITY BRIDGE AND TUNNEL AUTHORITY RULES

1. Vehicles carrying dangerous materials are not permitted in tunnels.
2. Overheight vehicles are not permitted in tunnels.
3. Overheight vehicles are not permitted on bridges.
4. Overweight vehicles are not permitted on bridges or in tunnels.
5. Dangerous materials are permitted on bridges, but only with a police escort.
6. All wide-load vehicles (vehicles whose overall width including load is greater than the width normally allowed) are refused passage through the tunnels.
7. Some wide-load vehicles are permitted on bridges, but only at specific times.

Times When Wide-Load Vehicles are Permitted on Bridges

Monday through Friday:	10 A.M. - 3 P.M.
	7 P.M. - 10 P.M.
Saturday and Sunday:	6 A.M. - 2 P.M.

3. A trailer truck driven by Sam Azure approaches a toll
   booth at the Burke Tunnel. The truck has a height of
   14 feet. The tunnel has a height of 13 feet 6 inches.
   The one of the following actions which the Bridge and
   Tunnel Officer on duty should take is to
     A. allow the truck to go through the tunnel
     B. detain the truck for two hours
     C. refuse to let the truck go through the tunnel
     D. direct the truck to a tunnel with 4 inches more
        clearance

      3.____

4. Tom Lynx, who is driving a vehicle with a wide load, wishes
   to cross the Franklin Bridge. He arrives at the bridge at
   9:30 on a Wednesday morning, but is stopped by the Bridge
   and Tunnel Officer on duty.
   Which one of the following is a valid reason for the
   Officer to stop Lynx?
   Wide-load vehicles are not permitted
     A. on bridges on weekdays
     B. on bridges without a police escort
     C. in tunnels or on bridges
     D. on bridges until 10 A.M. on Wednesdays

      4.____

5. The Asamera Trucking Company wants to have one of their
   wide-load vehicles cross the Dutchess Bridge on a Satur-
   day morning.
   Which one of the following is an appropriate time for
   their vehicle to cross the bridge?
     A. 6:30 AM   B. 3:30 PM   C. 10:15 PM   D. 12:45 AM

      5.____

6. A Blue Ribbon Trucking Company truck arrives at the toll
   lane of the Atlantic Bridge. Bridge and Tunnel Officer
   Foster asks the driver what the truck contains. He finds
   that the truck contains a highly corrosive and extremely
   dangerous material.
   Officer Foster should tell the truck driver to
     A. proceed across the bridge
     B. pay an extra toll
     C. wait for a police escort
     D. use the nearest tunnel

      6.____

7. On Monday, at 9:30 A.M., Ken Johnson, driving a truck
   belonging to the South Street Lumber Company, arrives at
   the Appian Way Tunnel. The truck is 12 feet 6 inches
   high, and 8 feet 2 inches wide. The Bridge and Tunnel
   Officer tells Mr. Johnson that his truck is too large to
   use that facility. However, the Officer considers
   either a tunnel or a bridge by which Johnson can reach
   his destination. The tunnel is 12 feet 5 inches high,
   and the bridge is 13 feet 1 inch high. The maximum width
   of a vehicle normally allowed in the tunnel is 8 feet
   6 inches. The maximum width of a vehicle normally allowed
   on the bridge is 8 feet 1 inch.

      7.____

Of the following, the Officer should tell Mr. Johnson to
    A. take the tunnel because it is wide enough and the bridge is not
    B. wait until 10 A.M. and then take the tunnel
    C. take the bridge because it is high enough and wide enough
    D. wait until 10 A.M. and then take the bridge

8. At which one of the following times will a wide-load vehicle be permitted on a bridge?   8.___
    A. 9 A.M. - Monday   B. 4 P.M. - Wednesday
    C. 6 A.M. - Friday   D. 1 P.M. - Sunday

9. A truck with which one of the following measurements would be allowed in a tunnel which is 13 feet 9 inches high and 9 feet 2 inches wide?   9.___
    13 feet _____ inches high and _____ feet _____ inches wide.
    A. 8; 9; 3   B. 10; 9; 4
    C. 11; 9; 0   D. 6; 8; 11

10. Al Levitt is driving a truck which is 11 feet 10 inches high, and 7 feet 11 inches wide. He must choose between a tunnel which is 12 feet 6 inches high and 8 feet 1 inch wide; and a bridge which is 15 feet 1 inch high and 7 feet 9 inches wide. He chooses to drive through the tunnel. His decision can BEST be described as   10.___
    A. *proper* because the tunnel is high enough and the bridge is not
    B. *improper* because the bridge is high enough and the tunnel is not
    C. *proper* because the tunnel is wide enough and the bridge is not
    D. *improper* because the bridge is wide enough and the tunnel is not

Questions 11-17.

DIRECTIONS: Questions 11 through 17 are to be answered SOLELY on the basis of the following information and form. Read the information, and look at the form before you begin answering the questions.

Certain government vehicles do not pay a toll. The Sloan City Bridge and Tunnel Authority has procedures concerning the completion of a form called a Non-Revenue Vehicle Report. Each Bridge and Tunnel Officer must record the time, license number, department, and lane number for each non-revenue vehicle using a facility.

The following is a list of vehicles that are non-revenue vehicles (vehicles which do not pay a toll):
    - Sloan City Police Department vehicle
    - Sloan City Fire Department vehicle
    - General Services Department vehicle
    - Air Pollution Control Department vehicle

Note that each line on this form is numbered from Line 1 to Line 8 for your reference.

SLOAN CITY BRIDGE AND TUNNEL AUTHORITY
NON-REVENUE VEHICLE REPORT

Officer: Henry Smith   Date: 12/2/89
Facility: Pike Tunnel   Toll Lane: Various

	TIME	LICENSE NUMBER	DEPARTMENT	LANE NUMBER
Line 1.		XYZ124	Fire Department	
Line 2.	9:18 A.M.		Police Department	12
Line 3.	10:05 A.M.	216OLA		14
Line 4.	11:16 A.M.		General Services Department	7
Line 5.	11:57 A.M.	365KCO		8
Line 6.	1:05 P.M.	356CKO		
Line 7.				
Line 8.	2:10 P.M.	653OCK	Air Pollution Control Department	17

11. At 9:18 A.M., an incomplete entry was made for a Police Department vehicle.
    What required information is missing from this line?
      A. Date   B. Department
      C. Lane Number   D. License Number   11.____

12. At 2:10 P.M., a vehicle with License Number 653OCK passed through the Pike Tunnel.
    According to the above report, that vehicle was from the _____ Department.
      A. General Services   B. Air Pollution Control
      C. Police   D. Fire   12.____

13. The information missing from both Line 1 and Line 6 is the
      A. Time   B. License Number
      C. Department   D. Lane Number   13.____

14. At 11:16 A.M., a General Services vehicle passed through Lane
      A. 7   B. 8   C. 12   D. 14   14.____

15. Which line in the above report is fully completed?
      A. 7   B. 8   C. 14   D. 17   15.____

16. What required information is missing from the line that includes License Number 216OLA?
      A. Date   B. Time
      C. Department   D. Lane Number   16.____

17. Which one of the following license numbers belongs to   17.___
    the Fire Department?
       A. 365KCO   B. 356CKO   C. 653OCK   D. XYZ124

Questions 18-24.

DIRECTIONS: Questions 18 through 24 are to be answered SOLELY on
              the basis of the information and the partially com-
              pleted Cash Deposit Record shown below.

    After the completion of a tour of duty, a Toll Collector is
required to tally and total all paper currency (bills) collected
during his tour and submit a Cash Deposit Report. This report
lists the bills by denomination, the number of bills, and the total
amount for each denomination.

    Note that each line on this form is lettered from A to Line G
for your reference.

BRIDGE AND TUNNEL AUTHORITY CASH DEPOSIT REPORT

	DENOMINATION	NUMBER	TOTAL AMOUNT OF CASH (in dollars)
Name of Officer: John Jones Date: 3/19/89 Facility: Yellowstone Bridge Tour: 9-5			
Line A	100		400
Line B	50		300
Line C	20	46	
Line D	10	64	
Line E	5		155
Line F	2	12	
Line G	1	786	

18. According to Officer Jones' Cash Deposit Report, the   18.___
    TOTAL amount of cash that should be entered on Line D is
       A. $220   B. $300   C. $640   D. $920

19. The figure that should be entered in the Number column on   19.___
    Line A is
       A. 3   B. 4   C. 5   D. 6

20. The TOTAL amount of cash that should be entered on Line C   20.___
    is
       A. $20   B. $46   C. $920   D. $1100

21. The missing entry on Line E is   21.___
       A. 25   B. 27   C. 29   D. 31

22. The missing entry on Line G should be   22.___
       A. 7   B. 78   C. 786   D. 78600

23. Officer Jones has collected twelve two-dollar bills during   23.____
    his tour. The total amount of these bills is $24.00.
    On what line should this entry appear?
    Line
    A. A   B. B   C. F   D. G

24. The figure that should be entered in the Number column on   24.____
    Line B is
    A. 6   B. 20   C. 50   D. 100

Questions 25-31.

DIRECTIONS: Bridge and Tunnel Officers may redirect lost cars, give
information, and issue summonses for both major and
minor traffic violations. Accuracy in completing the
summonses is very important. Questions 25 through 31
are to be answered SOLELY on the basis of the paragraphs
and the summons form below. Read the paragraphs and
look at the summons before answering the questions.

On March 2, 1989, at 7:34 A.M., Officer Natasha Seminoff observed
a vehicle with a blue and white Connecticut license plate No. 691ACF,
smoking excessively. The vehicle is a 1970 two-door red Chevrolet
sedan and is driven by a Mr. Richard Glenn. After checking Mr. Glenn's
license, registration, and insurance card, Officer Seminoff released
him without penalty, but with a stern warning to have his oil checked
immediately.

At 7:59 A.M., Officer Mike Haskell relieved Officer Natasha
Seminoff and assumed patrol duty. At 8:00 A.M., Officer Haskell
noticed a 1969 grey four-door Volvo sedan with New York license plate
number 619AFC. The registration on this car expired on October 31,
1988. Officer Haskell advised the driver, Mr. Allen Engels of
603 West 18th Street, New York, N.Y. 10031, of his violation.
Officer Haskell asked Mr. Engels for his license, registration, and
insurance card. The license and insurance card were valid. However,
although Mr. Engels was driving the car, the owner of the car was a
Mr. Morton Giller. Officer Haskell wrote out and issued the summons
to Mr. Engels at 8:19 A.M. After accepting the summons, Mr. Engels
was told that his court appearance date is on 4/22/89. Mr. Engels
thanked the officer and drove away.

SUMMONS

(Note that each line on this form is numbered from 1 to 24 for your reference.)

Line 1	Name:
Line 2	Address:
Line 3	City: State:
Line 4	Date of Birth:
Line 5	Male or Female:
Line 6	Driver's License Number:
Line 7	State Issuing License:
Line 8	Date License Expires:
Line 9	Make and Year of Vehicle:
Line 10	Body Type:
Line 11	Color of Vehicle:
Line 12	Owner of Vehicle:
Line 13	License Plate Number:
Line 14	State Issuing Plates:
Line 15	Date Plates Expire:
Line 16	Place of Violation:
Line 17	Violation:
Line 18	Date of Violation:
Line 19	Fine:
Line 20	Court Appearance Date:
Line 21	Summons Number: 89101122
Line 22	Signature of Officer Issuing Summons:
Line 23	Printed Name of Officer Issuing Summons:
Line 24	Time Summons is Issued:

25. On which one of the following lines should the date of   25.__
    the violation be entered?
    A. 8   B. 15   C. 18   D. 24

26. Which one of the following dates should be entered on   26.__
    Line 20?
    A. 10/31/88   B. 3/02/89   C. 3/20/89   D. 4/22/89

27. Which one of the following names should be entered on   27.__
    Line 1?
    A. Natasha Seminoff   B. Allen Engels
    C. Morton Giller   D. Mike Haskell

28. Which one of the following colors should be entered on   28.__
    Line 11?
    A. White   B. Grey   C. Blue   D. Red

29. Which one of the following times should be entered on   29.__
    Line 24?
    _____ A.M.
    A. 7:34   B. 7:59   C. 8:00   D. 8:19

30. Which one of the following license plate numbers should be entered on Line 13?   30.___
    A. 619AFC   B. 619FCA   C. 691ACF   D. 916CFA

31. Which one of the following vehicles should be entered on Line 9?   31.___
    A. 1970 Chevrolet   B. 1969 Volvo
    C. 1982 Chevrolet   D. 1981 Volvo

Questions 32-40.

DIRECTIONS: Questions 32 through 40 are to be answered SOLELY on the basis of the following rules.

BRIDGE AND TUNNEL AUTHORITY RULES

<u>Rule 100</u>.   When assigned to a lane, an Officer should proceed immediately to that lane and relieve the Officer stationed there.

<u>Rule 101</u>.   While on patrol, the Officer shall always be alert, observing everything that takes place within the Officer's sight or hearing.

<u>Rule 102</u>.   The Officer shall speak to patrons only in order to carry out his duties.

<u>Rule 103</u>.   An Officer is not permitted to leave his toll booth unless properly relieved or given permission by the Bridge and Tunnel Sergeant to close the toll booth.

<u>Rule 104</u>.   Employees are not permitted to smoke while on duty, unless in the lunchroom, restroom, or facility service building.

<u>Rule 105</u>.   An Officer shall give his or her name, rank, and badge number to any person who requests it.

<u>Rule 106</u>.   Officers are not permitted to ask patrons for rides.

<u>Rule 107</u>.   The official business of the Authority is to be treated as confidential. A request for other than strictly routine information must be referred to the Office of the Executive Officer.

<u>Rule 108</u>.   An Officer is not permitted to engage in betting on Authority property.

32. When an Officer is assigned to a lane, he should immediately go to the   32.___
    A. Administration Building
    B. Officer in the lane assigned
    C. closest unmanned toll booth
    D. Bridge and Tunnel Sergeant

33. An Officer is NOT allowed to smoke while on duty except   33.__
    when he is
    A. assigned to a plaza post
    B. in the toll booth
    C. assigned to a tunnel post
    D. in the lunchroom

34. At 11 P.M., an Officer assigned to a lane to collect toll   34.__
    on a 3 P.M. to 11 P.M. tour of duty should
    A. close his lane
    B. get permission from the Bridge and Tunnel Sergeant to
       close his lane
    C. call the Desk Officer for permission to close his lane
    D. ask the plaza post man to collect tolls

35. A motorist is angry because of a delay while traveling   35.__
    through a Bridge and Tunnel Authority tunnel. When the
    motorist arrives at the toll booth, he asks the Officer
    on duty his name and badge number.
    The Officer should
    A. tell the motorist delays are normal
    B. give his name and badge number
    C. call for the Bridge and Tunnel Sergeant
    D. direct the motorist to the Office of the Executive
       Officer

36. While assigned as Desk Officer, Officer Ely receives a   36.__
    call from a local newspaper reporter inquiring about a
    rumored increase in tolls.
    Officer Ely should
    A. tell the reporter the toll is going up
    B. tell the reporter the toll is not going up
    C. refer the reporter to the Office of the Controller
    D. refer the reporter to the Office of the Executive
       Officer

37. During his tour of duty, an Officer should ALWAYS be   37.__
    aware of
    A. every occurrence within his sight or hearing
    B. the total amount of money he collected the previous
       day
    C. what his Bridge and Tunnel Sergeant is doing
    D. the location of all fellow Officers

38. An Officer wishes to go from one location in a tunnel to   38.__
    another. However, he does not have an immediate means of
    transportation.
    From which one of the following is an Officer prohibited?
    A. Using the Bridge and Tunnel Lieutenant's car with
       permission
    B. Asking a patron for a ride
    C. Getting a ride in the tow truck assigned to the tunnel
    D. Waiting until an official means of transportation is
       made available

39. An Officer at a facility decides he would like to take   39.____
    bets on football games.
    According to the rules, this employee is ____ to accept
    bets because ____.
    A. allowed; it is his private business
    B. not allowed; betting is prohibited
    C. not allowed; some employees may lose money
    D. allowed; someone may get lucky

40. On a Sunday afternoon, Raquel Summers, a motorist, drives   40.____
    up to Officer Brown's toll booth. After paying her toll,
    Ms. Summers, instead of driving off, begins to talk to
    the Officer about the coming World Series.
    In this case, Officer Brown should
    A. politely ask Ms. Summers to drive on
    B. continue speaking with Ms. Summers since the Officer
       is not busy
    C. continue speaking with Ms. Summers since an Officer
       is required to be polite to motorists
    D. tell Ms. Summers that he is not a baseball fan, but
       that he would be happy to discuss golf or tennis

KEY (CORRECT ANSWERS)

1. D	11. D	21. D	31. B
2. C	12. B	22. C	32. B
3. C	13. D	23. C	33. D
4. D	14. A	24. A	34. B
5. A	15. B	25. C	35. B
6. C	16. C	26. D	36. D
7. D	17. D	27. B	37. A
8. D	18. C	28. B	38. B
9. D	19. B	29. D	39. B
10. C	20. C	30. A	40. A

READING COMPREHENSION
UNDERSTANDING AND INTERPRETING WRITTEN MATERIAL
EXAMINATION SECTION
TEST 1

DIRECTIONS: Each question or incomplete statement is followed by several suggested answers or completions. Select the one that BEST answers the question or completes the statement. *PRINT THE LETTER OF THE CORRECT ANSWER IN THE SPACE AT THE RIGHT.*

Questions 1-4.

DIRECTIONS: Questions 1 through 4 are to be answered SOLELY on the basis of the following paragraph.

When a vehicle has been disabled in the tunnel, the officer on patrol in this zone shall press the emergency truck light button. In the fast lane, red lights will go on throughout the tunnel; in the slow lane, amber lights will go on throughout the tunnel. The yellow zone light will go on at each signal control station throughout the tunnel and will flash the number of the zone in which the stoppage has occurred. A red flashing pilot light will appear only at the signal control station at which the emergency truck button was pressed. The emergency garage will receive an audible and visual signal indicating the signal control station at which the emergency truck button was pressed. The garage officer shall acknowledge receipt of the signal by pressing the acknowledgment button. This will cause the pilot light at the operated signal control station in the tunnel to cease flashing and to remain steady. It is an answer to the officer at the operated signal control station that the emergency truck is responding to the call.

1. According to this paragraph, when the emergency truck light button is pressed,   1.___
    A. amber lights will go on in every lane throughout the tunnel
    B. emergency signal lights will go on only in the lane in which the disabled vehicle happens to be
    C. red lights will go on in the fast lane throughout the tunnel
    D. pilot lights at all signal control stations will turn amber

2. According to this paragraph, the number of the zone in which the stoppage has occurred is flashed   2.___
    A. immediately after all the lights in the tunnel turn red
    B. by the yellow zone light at each signal control station
    C. by the emergency truck at the point of stoppage
    D. by the emergency garage

3. According to this paragraph, an officer near the disabled vehicle will know that the emergency tow truck is coming when   3.___
    A. the pilot light at the operated signal control station appears and flashes red

B. an audible signal is heard in the tunnel
C. the zone light at the operated signal control station turns red
D. the pilot light at the operated signal control station becomes steady

4. Under the system described in the paragraph, it would be CORRECT to come to the conclusion that
    A. officers at all signal control stations are expected to acknowledge that they have received the stoppage signal
    B. officers at all signal control stations will know where the stoppage has occurred
    C. all traffic in both lanes of that side of the tunnel in which the stoppage has occurred must stop until the emergency truck has arrived
    D. there are two emergency garages, each able to respond to stoppages in traffic going in one particular direction

4.___

Questions 5-8.

DIRECTIONS: Questions 5 through 8 are to be answered SOLELY on the basis of the information given in the paragraph below.

A summons is an official statement ordering a person to appear in court. In traffic violation situations, summonses are used when arrests need not be made. The main reason for traffic summonses is to deter motorists from repeating the same traffic violation. Occasionally, motorists may make unintentional driving errors, and sometimes they are unaware of correct driving regulations. In cases such as these, the policy should be to have the officer verbally inform the motorist of the violation and warn him against repeating it. The purpose of this practice is not to limit the number of summonses, but rather to prevent the issuing of summonses when the violation is not due to deliberate intent or to inexcusable negligence.

5. According to the above paragraph, the PRINCIPAL reason for issuing traffic summonses is to
    A. discourage motorists from violating these laws again
    B. increase the money collected by the city
    C. put traffic violators in prison
    D. have them serve as substitutes for police officers

5.___

6. The reason a verbal warning may sometimes be substituted for a summons is to
    A. limit the number of summonses
    B. distinguish between excusable and inexcusable violations
    C. provide harsher penalties for deliberate intent than for inexcusable negligence
    D. decrease the caseload in the courts

6.___

7. The above paragraph implies that someone who violated a   7.____
   traffic regulation because he did NOT know about the
   regulation should be
      A. put under arrest   B. fined less money
      C. given a summons   D. told not to do it again

8. Using the distinctions made by the above paragraph, the   8.____
   one of the following motorists to whom it would be MOST
   desirable to issue a summons is the one who exceeded the
   speed limit because he
      A. did not know the speed limit
      B. was late for an important business appointment
      C. speeded to avoid being hit by another car
      D. had a speedometer which was not working properly

Questions 9-11.

DIRECTIONS: Questions 9 through 11 are to be answered in accordance
                with the paragraphs below.

The proper use of artificial respiration is of the greatest
importance when breathing has stopped in cases of electric shock,
gas poisoning, or drowning.

The first minutes in applying artificial respiration are most
important. It should start immediately and be continued without
interruption (if necessary for four hours) until natural breathing
is restored. Someone else should call the doctor.

The first step in cases of electric shock is to instantly
break the contact. Any available non-conductor can be used for
this purpose, but the hands of the individual applying artificial
respiration must be protected to avoid further accident (if possible,
shut off the current or break the circuit).

The victim of gas poisoning must immediately receive fresh air,
preferably in a warm dry atmosphere. Use proper protective equipment before entering gas-filled atmosphere. If such equipment is
not available, hold your breath while you dash in and drag out the
victim.

9. In cases of electric shock, the FIRST step to take is to   9.____
      A. lay the victim face down and start artificial respira-
         tion
      B. give the victim a stimulant
      C. break the contact with the live circuit
      D. put a blanket over the victim

10. In cases of gas poisoning, the FIRST step to take is to   10.____
       A. lay the victim face down and take foreign objects
          out of his mouth
       B. give the victim a stimulant
       C. cover the victim with blankets
       D. take the victim out of the gas-filled atmosphere and
          into the fresh air

11. Artificial respiration should be continued   11.___
    A. for half an hour *only*
    B. for two or three hours *only*
    C. until the victim's face becomes flushed
    D. until the victim's natural breathing is restored or
       a physician tells you to stop

Questions 12-15.

DIRECTIONS: Questions 12 through 15 are to be answered in accordance
           with the paragraphs below.

Lay the victim face down, with one arm extended directly over-
head, the other arm bent at the elbow with his face turned outward
resting on hand or forearm to keep nose and mouth free for breathing.
Kneel straddling the victim's hips with the knees just below the
patient's hip bones. Place your palms on the small of his back,
with fingers on ribs, little finger just touching the lowest rib.
This is important as placing fingers too high may cause a rib injury;
placing them too low puts pressure on kidneys where it does no good
and may do harm.

Swing forward gradually bringing your weight to bear. Keep arms
stiff. Shoulders should be directly over back of hand. After about
two seconds, release pressure gradually by swinging back on your
heels and letting hands drop. Repeat this sequence of operations
smoothly and rhythmically.

While you continue artificial respiration, any helpers you may
have should take any foreign objects (if any) out of the victim's
mouth, cover him with blankets or coats, and send for a doctor
immediately.

12. In applying artificial respiration, you should kneel   12.___
    straddling the victim with your knees
    A. just below the shoulders
    B. halfway between the small of the back and the shoulders
    C. midway between the mid-point of the thighs and the knees
    D. just below the hip bones

13. One of the MOST important reasons why the hands should not   13.___
    be placed too low in applying artificial respiration is
    that this
    A. may result in a broken rib
    B. may injure the liver
    C. does no good
    D. is likely to cause the victim to inhale when he
       should exhale

14. In applying artificial respiration, you should swing   14.___
    forward
    A. quickly with arms stiff
    B. quickly with arms bent
    C. gradually with arms bent
    D. gradually with arms stiff

15. While you are giving artificial respiration, your   15.____
    assistants should
        A. give the victim a stimulant and cover him with
           blankets immediately
        B. take foreign objects out of the victim's mouth and
           give him a stimulant immediately
        C. dash water in his face and give him a drink of
           water immediately
        D. take foreign objects out of his mouth and send for
           a doctor immediately

Questions 16-23.

DIRECTIONS: Questions 16 through 23 are to be answered ONLY on the
               basis of the Rules for Bridge and Tunnel Officers given
               below.

RULES FOR BRIDGE AND TUNNEL OFFICERS

   I. Officers shall give their name, rank, and badge number to any
      person who requests it.
  II. An officer on duty at a tunnel post shall immediately press
      the button for fire, obstructed lane, or dangerous vehicle
      when one of these conditions exist.
 III. If the driver of a vehicle does not have the cash or stamped
      ticket to pay a toll, he shall not be allowed to use the
      facility.
  IV. An officer shall permit only authorized persons on official
      business to be in a toll booth or at a tunnel post.
   V. An officer in a toll booth shall get assistance from his
      supervisor in any situation when he is unsure whether a
      vehicle should be allowed to proceed.

16. An officer collects the correct toll from a truck driver.   16.____
    However, the driver says that bridge tolls are too high
    and in an angry voice asks the officer for his name and
    number so that he can write a letter about the high tolls.
    Of the following, the BEST thing for the officer to do
    is to
        A. tell the driver that he is holding up traffic and
           should move on
        B. give his name and badge number to the driver
        C. tell the driver not to use the bridge anymore if the
           toll is too high
        D. provide the driver with reasons for the tolls charged

17. While on duty at a post in a tunnel, an officer notices   17.____
    a driver putting out a small fire in the engine of a car.
    At that moment, the driver turns to the officer and yells,
    I can put it out myself.
    The FIRST thing the officer should do is
        A. help the driver put out the fire
        B. press the button which signals a fire in the tunnel
        C. let the motorist handle the situation himself
        D. call his supervisor and ask for help

18. A motorist approaching a bridge stops at a toll booth   18.____
    and hands the officer postage stamps instead of coins
    to pay the toll.
    The officer should FIRST
    A. refuse the stamps and tell the driver that the bridge
       toll must be paid in cash
    B. accept the stamps as payment of the toll
    C. request assistance in dealing with the situation
    D. refuse the stamps, let the vehicle go on, but have
       the driver promise that he will return with the money

19. An officer at a post inside a tunnel sees two large   19.____
    cartons fall off a truck.
    The officer's FIRST response should be to
    A. try to move the cartons to the side of the roadway
    B. signal another officer to stop the truck at the
       tunnel's exit
    C. run after the truck to tell the driver what has
       happened
    D. use an appropriate signal button

20. Suppose that, while an officer is collecting tolls, a   20.____
    car stops at the toll booth and the driver appears to be
    drunk.
    Of the following, the FIRST thing the officer should do
    is to
    A. tell the driver to proceed very carefully and be sure
       not to drive after drinking in the future
    B. signal another officer to assist him in escorting the
       driver to their supervisor
    C. refuse to accept the toll money and call his super-
       visor
    D. immediately press the emergency button

21. While on duty inside a tunnel, an officer notices that a   21.____
    car has stopped and has a flat tire. It is late evening,
    and there is no other traffic visible.
    The FIRST thing the officer should do is to
    A. quickly assist the driver in changing the tire
    B. signal that a lane is blocked
    C. tell the driver to drive out of the tunnel
    D. issue a summons to the motorist for stopping his
       car inside a tunnel

22. Suppose that a friend tells an officer that he is   22.____
    interested in learning about the officer's work. The
    friend says that he would like to visit the officer in
    a toll booth for an hour the next day.
    Of the following, which one is the BEST reply for the
    officer to make?
    A. Sorry, but I'm not allowed to let you in the booth.
    B. You can stay in the booth, but be careful not to
       touch anything
    C. You can't come inside the booth, but you can stay
       with me in the tunnel.
    D. It's all right, but be sure to give my name, rank,
       and number if anyone questions you.

23. Assume that, while an officer is collecting a toll from   23.____
    a motorist, the officer sees a child tied up in the rear
    of the car.
    Of the following, the BEST thing for the officer to do
    is to
    A. ignore what he has seen and continue collecting tolls
    B. try to delay the car and signal for assistance
    C. reach into the car and untie the child
    D. tell the driver that he cannot use the bridge unless
       he unties the child

Questions 24-30.

DIRECTIONS: Questions 24 through 30 are to be answered SOLELY on
            the basis of the information contained in the following
            paragraphs.

Snow-covered roads spell trouble for motorists all winter long.
Clearing highways of snow and ice to keep millions of motor vehicles
moving freely is a tremendous task. Highway departments now rely,
to a great extent, on chemical deicers to get the big job done.
Sodium chloride, in the form of commercial salt, is the deicer most
frequently used.

There is no reliable evidence to prove that salt reduces highway
accidents. But available statistics are impressive. For example,
before Massachusetts used chemical deicers, it had a yearly average
of 21 fatal accidents and 1,635 injuries attributed to cars skidding
on snow or ice. Beginning in 1940, the state began fighting hazardous driving conditions with chemical deicers. During the period
1940-50, there was a yearly average of only seven deaths and 736
injuries as a result of skids.

Economical and effective in a moderately low temperature range,
salt is increasingly popular with highway departments, but not so
popular with individual car owners. Salty slush eats away at metal,
including auto bodies. It also sprinkles windshields with a fine-
grained spray which dries on contact, severely reducing visibility.
However, drivers who are hindered or immobilized by heavy winter
weather favor the liberal use of products such as sodium chloride.
When snow blankets roads, these drivers feel that the quickest way
to get back to the safety of driving on bare pavement is through
use of deicing salts.

24. The MAIN reason given by the above passage for the use   24.____
    of sodium chloride as a deicer is that it
    A. has no harmful side effects
    B. is economical
    C. is popular among car owners
    D. reduces highway accidents

25. The above passage may BEST be described as a(n)   25.____
    A. argument against the use of sodium chloride as a
       deicer
    B. discussion of some advantages and disadvantages of
       sodium chloride as a deicer

C. recommendation to use sodium chloride as a deicer
D. technical account of the uses and effects of sodium chloride as a deicer

26. Based on the above passage, the use of salt on snow-covered roadways will EVENTUALLY   26._____
    A. decrease the efficiency of the automotive fuel
    B. cause tires to deteriorate
    C. damage the surface of the roadway
    D. cause holes in the sides of cars

27. The AVERAGE number of persons killed yearly in Massachu-   27._____
    setts in car accidents caused by skidding on snow or ice
    before chemical deicers were used there was
       A. 9   B. 12   C. 21   D. 30

28. According to the passage, it would be ADVISABLE to use   28._____
    salt as a deicer when
       A. outdoor temperatures are somewhat below freezing
       B. residues on highway surfaces are deemed to be
          undesirable
       C. snow and ice have low absorbency characteristics
       D. the use of a substance is desired which dries on
          contact

29. As a result of using chemical deicers, the number of   29._____
    injuries resulting from skids in Massachusetts was
    reduced by about
       A. 35%   B. 45%   C. 55%   D. 65%

30. According to the above passage, driver visibility can   30._____
    be severely reduced by
       A. sodium chloride deposits on the windshield
       B. glare from salt and snow crystals
       C. salt spray covering the front lights
       D. faulty windshield wipers

KEY (CORRECT ANSWERS)

1. C	11. D	21. B
2. B	12. D	22. A
3. D	13. C	23. B
4. B	14. D	24. B
5. A	15. D	25. B
6. B	16. B	26. D
7. D	17. B	27. C
8. B	18. A	28. A
9. C	19. D	29. C
10. D	20. C	30. A

TEST 2

DIRECTIONS: Each question or incomplete statement is followed by
                several suggested answers or completions. Select the
                one that BEST answers the question or completes the
                statement. *PRINT THE LETTER OF THE CORRECT ANSWER IN
                THE SPACE AT THE RIGHT.*

Questions 1-3.

DIRECTIONS: Questions 1 through 3 are to be answered according to the
                information contained in the following paragraph.

        Each parking meter collector shall keep a permanently-bound
notebook record of each day's field activities, noting therein the
date, area, and the numbers of the meters from which collections
were made or which were serviced by him. While at the meter, he
shall also note therein any reason why a coin box was not collected
or bulk revenue was not collected; the number and denominations of
all loose coins found in the coin compartment of a coin box meter;
those meters which are damaged in any respect and the nature of such
damage; why a meter was not placed in operation; and any other
information or circumstance which may affect the collections,
revenue, operation or maintenance of the meters he serviced. Any
damage to collection equipment and the nature of the damage shall
also be noted in such book. All such notations shall be set forth
on the prescribed daily report form to be made out by the employee
at the conclusion of each day's assignment. Said report shall be
signed by all of the members of the collection crew.

1. The term *bulk revenue* in the above passage MOST probably   1.____
   refers to
       A. money not in a coin box
       B. money in a coin box
       C. money not taken from a meter
       D. paper money

2. A parking meter collector finds 60¢ in loose coins   2.____
   (3 nickels, 2 dimes, 1 quarter) in the coin compartment
   of a coin box meter.
   Of the following, the BEST way to enter this in his notebook is *loose coins*
       A. 60¢
       B. 2 dimes, 3 nickels, 1 quarter
       C. 6, 60¢ total
       D. 3 Jefferson nickels, 2 Roosevelt dimes, 1 Washington
          quarter

3. The parking meter collector's daily report form is MAINLY   3.____
   intended to be used to report the
       A. activities of collection crews with more than one or
          two members
       B. information not recorded in the bound notebook
       C. information recorded in the bound notebook
       D. unusual occurrences of the day

Questions 4-12.

DIRECTIONS: Questions 4 through 12 are to be answered according to the
               rules listed below.

RULES FOR BRIDGE OPERATION

When a vessel owned by the U.S. Government or the city approaches
a movable bridge, it shall signal with four *distinct* blasts of a
whistle.
All other vessels signal with three distinct blasts of a whistle.
All call signals for openings shall be answered promptly by the
bridge by 2 long distinct blasts.
This signal indicates to the boat that the call signal has been
heard, and preparations to open will be made.
After this signal, the Bridge Operator shall open his bridge at
such a time which in his judgment and experience will permit *prompt*
passage of the boat without unreasonable delay and will not create
any unreasonable delay to land traffic.
At no time shall the draw be moved until all sidewalk and roadway traffic gates are locked in their closed position.
If the draw cannot be opened, the 2 blast signal shall be
repeated until acknowledged by the boat.
It is *extremely* important that the draw be brought to its fully
opened position at all times, irrespective of the size of the boat.
(This does not apply to test openings.)
When the draw is fully opened, the Bridge Operator shall sound
the same signal as the call signal.
While the draw is in its fully opened position, no attempt shall
be made toward closing until the passing boat has cleared the draw.
Except in rare emergencies, the draw shall not be moved either
in closing or opening while there is a boat in the draw.
When the draw is fully closed and land traffic can be resumed,
the Bridge Operator is to sound one blast which will be the signal
for the Bridge Tenders to open all traffic gates.
Visual signals shall be used as prescribed by the Department of
the Army whenever sound signals cannot be given or if sound signals
cannot be heard.
The time of an opening shall be the *interval* between the time
the traffic gates are closed and the time they are opened.

4. As used above, *prompt* means MOST NEARLY   4.___
       A. easy   B. safe   C. speedy   D. careful

5. As used above, *extremely* means MOST NEARLY   5.___
       A. very   B. mildly   C. of course   D. sometimes

6. As used above, *visual* means MOST NEARLY   6.___
       A. telegraph B. bell   C. runner   D. sight

7. According to the above statements, if an approaching   7.___
    vessel signals for an opening with 4 blasts, it means
    that the vessel is
       A. a tanker   B. a tug
       C. foreign-owned   D. city-owned

8. According to the above rules, a boat approaching a bridge   8.___
   will signal the bridge by
       A. swinging a red light
       B. calling through a megaphone
       C. blowing a whistle
       D. waving a blue flag

9. According to the above rules, the bridge answers the boat   9.___
   by blowing a whistle
       A. once   B. twice
       C. three times   D. four times

10. According to the above rules, when a bridge is opened for   10.___
    passage of a boat, the amount that the bridge is opened
    will
        A. vary, depending on the size of boat *only*
        B. vary, depending on the tide *only*
        C. vary, depending on the size of boat and the tide
        D. always be the same

11. According to the above rules, the operator NORMALLY will   11.___
    begin to close the bridge
        A. as soon as the boat enters the draw, so the operator
           knows the height of the boat
        B. when the center of the boat has passed the center of
           the bridge
        C. at any time convenient to the operator
        D. after the boat has completely passed through the draw

12. According to the above rules, the man operating the   12.___
    traffic gate knows the bridge is closed when he
        A. sees the bridge operator wave
        B. sees the traffic signals turn green
        C. feels the bridge come together
        D. hears a single blast on a whistle

Questions 13-16.

DIRECTIONS: Questions 13 through 16 are to be answered according to
              the information contained in the following paragraph.

When reporting for work each day, an assistant bridge operator
is required to sign his time card. At this time, he will read the
notices published on the bulletin board for any changes in rules or
special conditions that may affect him. After changing into work
clothes, the supervisor will assign the assistant bridge operator
to any work that has to be done. When the bridge is not open, there
may be tasks such as cleaning the motor room, oiling the machinery
or minor repair work. When the bridge is to be opened, the assistant
bridge operator will go to his post at one end of the bridge and will
signal all traffic to stop by means of lights. Immediately thereafter,
he will start to lower the barricades. However, the barricades will
not be completely lowered until all traffic has stopped. The bridge
is then opened.

13. According to the above paragraph, the FIRST thing an   13.____
    assistant bridge operator does when reporting for work is
    to
       A. read the bulletin board
       B. change to work clothes
       C. sign his time card
       D. report to his supervisor

14. The purpose of reading the bulletin board is to   14.____
       A. find out what work has to be done
       B. see who the supervisor is
       C. save time
       D. be aware of any changes in rules

15. Work to which the assistant bridge operator may be assigned 15.____
    is
       A. oiling the motors
       B. hand signalling traffic
       C. replacing the lift cables
       D. opening the bridge

16. Lowering of the barricades is begun   16.____
       A. before signalling the traffic to stop
       B. at the same time as the traffic is signalled to stop
       C. immediately after the traffic is signalled to stop
       D. after all traffic has stopped

Questions 17-30.

DIRECTIONS: Questions 17 through 30 are to be answered according to
             the information contained in the paragraph below.

      At 8:30 A.M. on Friday, February 2, 1979, Assistant Bridge
Operator Henry Jones started to clean the walk of the Avenue X Bridge.
It was snowing heavily, and the surface of the road was slippery.
At 8:32 A.M., Mr. Jones saw a westbound station wagon skid and strike
a westbound sedan about 50 feet from the barrier. Both cars were
badly damaged. The station wagon was overturned and came to rest
8 feet from the barrier. The woman driver of the station wagon,
Mrs. Harriet White, was thrown clear and landed in the middle of the
road. The other car was smashed against the barrier. The driver of
the sedan, Mr. Tom Green, was pinned behind the steering wheel and
suffered cuts about the face. Mr. Jones called the Bridge Operator,
Mr. Frank Smith, who telephoned for an ambulance. First aid was
given to both drivers. They were taken to the Avenue W Hospital by
an ambulance which was driven by Mr. James Doe and arrived on the
scene at 9:07 A.M. Patrolman John Brown, Badge No. 71162, had
arrived before the ambulance and recorded all the details of the
accident, including the statements of Mr. Henry Jones and of Mr. Jack
Black, another eyewitness.

17. The accident occurred on   17.____
       A. Saturday, February 3, 1978
       B. Friday, February 2, 1978
       C. Friday, February 2, 1979
       D. Friday, February 3, 1979

18. The time of the accident was   18.___
    A. 7:32 A.M.   B. 8:32 A.M.
    C. 8:32 P.M.   D. 7:32 P.M.

19. The Assistant Bridge Operator's name was   19.___
    A. Frank Smith   B. Tom Jones
    C. Henry Smith   D. Henry Jones

20. The accident involved a ____ and ____.   20.___
    A. sedan; a station wagon
    B. station wagon; a panel truck
    C. station wagon; two sedans
    D. sedan; two station wagons

21. The man named Jack Black was a(n)   21.___
    A. patrolman   B. eyewitness
    C. ambulance driver   D. street cleaner

22. The time which elapsed between the accident and the   22.___
    arrival of the ambulance was MOST NEARLY ____ minutes.
    A. 7   B. 28   C. 32   D. 35

23. The weather was   23.___
    A. fair   B. rainy   C. sleety   D. snowy

24. The station wagon was driven by   24.___
    A. Jane Brown   B. Jane White
    C. Harriet White   D. Harriet Brown

25. Tom Green was the   25.___
    A. driver of the ambulance B. driver of the sedan
    C. other eyewitness   D. patrolman

26. The barrier was   26.___
    A. struck by the sedan
    B. struck by the station wagon
    C. struck by both cars
    D. not struck by either car

27. The damage done to   27.___
    A. both cars was slight
    B. the sedan was severe but that done to the station
       wagon was slight
    C. the station wagon was severe but that done to the
       sedan was slight
    D. both cars was severe

28. The woman driver   28.___
    A. was pinned behind the wheel
    B. suffered face cuts
    C. was thrown clear
    D. was trapped in the car

29. The name of the Bridge Operator was   29.___
    A. Frank Smith   B. John Smith
    C. Henry Jones   D. Frank Jones

30. When the accident occurred, the _____ feet from the barrier.
    A. station wagon was 20   B. cars were 50
    C. sedan was 60   D. sedan was 8

30.____

_____

KEY (CORRECT ANSWERS)

1. A	11. D	21. B
2. B	12. D	22. D
3. C	13. C	23. D
4. C	14. D	24. C
5. A	15. A	25. B
6. D	16. C	26. A
7. D	17. C	27. D
8. C	18. B	28. C
9. B	19. D	29. A
10. D	20. A	30. B

_____

ARITHMETIC
EXAMINATION SECTION

DIRECTIONS: Each question or incomplete statement is followed by
several suggested answers or completions. Select the
one that BEST answers the question or completes the
statement. *PRINT THE LETTER OF THE CORRECT ANSWER IN
THE SPACE AT THE RIGHT.*

1. The sum of 53632 + 27403 + 98765 + 75424 is   1.___
   A. 19214   B. 215214   C. 235224   D. 255224

2. The sum of 76342 + 49050 + 21206 + 59989 is   2.___
   A. 196586   B. 206087   C. 206587   D. 234487

3. The sum of $452.13 + $963.45 + $621.25 is   3.___
   A. $1936.83   B. $2036.83   C. $2095.73 D. $2135.73

4. The sum of 36392 + 42156 + 98765 is   4.___
   A. 167214   B. 177203   C. 177313   D. 178213

5. The sum of 40125 + 87123 + 24689 is   5.___
   A. 141827   B. 151827   C. 151937   D. 161947

6. The sum of 2379 + 4015 + 6521 + 9986 is   6.___
   A. 22901   B. 22819   C. 21801   D. 21791

7. From 50962 subtract 36197.   7.___
   The answer should be
   A. 14675   B. 14765   C. 14865   D. 24765

8. From 90000 subtract 31928.   8.___
   The answer should be
   A. 58072   B. 59062   C. 68172   D. 69182

9. From 63764 subtract 21548.   9.___
   The answer should be
   A. 42216   B. 43122   C. 45126   D. 85312

10. From $9605.13 subtract $2715.96.   10.___
    The answer should be
    A. $12,321.09   B. $8,690.16
    C. $6,990.07   D. $6,889.17

11. From 76421 subtract 73101.   11.___
    The answer should be
    A. 3642   B. 3540   C. 3320   D. 3242

12. From $8.25 subtract $6.50.   12.___
    The answer should be
    A. $1.25   B. $1.50   C. $1.75   D. $2.25

13. Multiply 563 by 0.50.
    The answer should be
        A. 281.50   B. 28.15   C. 2.815   D. 0.2815
                 13.___

14. Multiply 0.35 by 1045.
    The answer should be
        A. 0.36575   B. 3.6575   C. 36.575   D. 365.75
                 14.___

15. Multiply 25 by 2513.
    The answer should be
        A. 62825   B. 62725   C. 60825   D. 52825
                 15.___

16. Multiply 423 by 0.01.
    The answer should be
        A. 0.0423   B. 0.423   C. 4.23   D. 42.3
                 16.___

17. Multiply 6.70 by 3.2.
    The answer should be
        A. 2.1440   B. 21.440   C. 214.40   D. 2144.0
                 17.___

18. Multiply 630 by 517.
    The answer should be
        A. 325,710   B. 345,720   C. 362,425   D. 385,660
                 18.___

19. Multiply 35 by 846.
    The answer should be
        A. 4050   B. 9450   C. 18740   D. 29610
                 19.___

20. Multiply 823 by 0.05.
    The answer should be
        A. 0.4115   B. 4.115   C. 41.15   D. 411.50
                 20.___

21. Multiply 1690 by 0.10.
    The answer should be
        A. 0.169   B. 1.69   C. 16.90   D. 169.0
                 21.___

22. Divide 2765 by 35.
    The answer should be
        A. 71   B. 79   C. 87   D. 93
                 22.___

23. From $18.55 subtract $6.80.
    The answer should be
        A. $9.75   B. $10.95   C. $11.75   D. $25.35
                 23.___

24. The sum of 2.75 + 4.50 + 3.60 is
        A. 9.75   B. 10.85   C. 11.15   D. 11.95
                 24.___

25. The sum of 9.63 + 11.21 + 17.25 is
        A. 36.09   B. 38.09   C. 39.92   D. 41.22
                 25.___

26. The sum of 112.0 + 16.9 + 3.84 is
        A. 129.3   B. 132.74   C. 136.48   D. 167.3
                 26.___

27. When 65 is added to the result of 14 multiplied by 13, the answer is
    A. 92   B. 182   C. 247   D. 16055

27.___

28. From $391.55 subtract $273.45.
    The answer should be
    A. $118.10   B. $128.20   C. $178.10   D. $218.20

28.___

29. When 119 is subtracted from the sum of 2016 + 1634, the answer is
    A. 2460   B. 3531   C. 3650   D. 3769

29.___

30. What is $367.20 + $510.00 + $402.80?
    A. $1,276.90 B. $1,277.90 C. $1,279.00 D. $1,280.00

30.___

31. Multiply 35 x 65 x 15.
    The answer should be
    A. 2275   B. 24265   C. 31145   D. 34125

31.___

32. Multiply 40 x 65 x 10.
    The answer should be
    A. 26000   B. 28000   C. 25200   D. 22300

32.___

33. The total amount of money represented by 43 half-dollars, 26 quarters, and 71 dimes is
    A. $28.00   B. $35.10   C. $44.30   D. $56.60

33.___

34. The total amount of money represented by 132 quarters, 97 dimes, and 220 nickels is
    A. $43.70   B. $44.20   C. $52.90   D. $53.70

34.___

35. The total amount of money represented by 40 quarters, 40 dimes, and 20 nickels is
    A. $14.50   B. $15.00   C. $15.50   D. $16.00

35.___

36. The sum of $29.61 + $101.53 + $943.64 is
    A. $983.88   B. $1074.78   C. $1174.98   D. $1341.42

36.___

37. The sum of $132.25 + $85.63 + $7056.44 is
    A. $1694.19   B. $7274.32   C. $8464.57   D. $9346.22

37.___

38. The sum of 4010 + 1271 + 23 + 838 is
    A. 6142   B. 6162   C. 6242   D. 6362

38.___

39. What is the value of 3 twenty dollar bills, 5 ten dollar bills, 13 five dollar bills, and 43 one dollar bills?
    A. $218.00   B. $219.00   C. $220.00   D. $221.00

39.___

40. What is the value of 8 twenty dollar bills, 13 ten dollar bills, 27 five dollar bills, 3 two dollar bills, and 43 one dollar bills?
    A. $364.00   B. $374.00   C. $474.00   D. $485.00

40.___

41. What is the value of 6 twenty dollar bills, 8 ten dollar
    bills, 19 five dollar bills, and 37 one dollar bills?   41.___
    A. $232.00   B. $233.00   C. $332.00   D. $333.00

42. What is the value of 13 twenty dollar bills, 17 ten dollar   42.___
    bills, 24 five dollar bills, 7 two dollar bills, and
    55 one dollar bills?
    A. $594.00   B. $599.00   C. $609.00   D. $619.00

43. What is the value of 7 half dollars, 9 quarters, 23 dimes,   43.___
    and 17 nickels?
    A. $7.80   B. $7.90   C. $8.80   D. $8.90

44. What is the value of 3 one dollar coins, 3 half dollars,   44.___
    7 quarters, 13 dimes, and 27 nickels?
    A. $7.80   B. $8.70   C. $8.80   D. $8.90

45. What is the value of 73 quarters?   45.___
    A. $18.25   B. $18.50   C. $18.75   D. $19.00

46. What is the value of 173 nickels?   46.___
    A. $8.55   B. $8.65   C. $8.75   D. $8.85

47. In checking a book of consecutively numbered Senior   47.___
    Citizen tickets, you find there are no tickets between
    number 13,383 and 13,833.
    How many tickets are missing?
    A. 448   B. 449   C. 450   D. 451

48. A ticket clerk begins her shift with 2,322 tickets.   48.___
    How many tickets will she have at the end of her shift
    if she sells 1,315 and collects 1,704 from the turn-
    stiles during her shift?
    A. 2,687   B. 2,693   C. 2,711   D. 2,722

49. A ticket clerk has three books of tickets. One contains   49.___
    273 tickets, one contains 342 tickets, and one contains
    159 tickets. The clerk combines the contents of the
    three books and then sells 217 tickets.
    How many tickets are left?
    A. 556   B. 557   C. 568   D. 991

50. A ticket clerk has a quantity of consecutively numbered   50.___
    tickets. The number on the ticket having the lowest
    number is 27,069. The number on the ticket having the
    highest number is 27,154.
    How many tickets does the clerk have?
    A. 84   B. 85   C. 86   D. 87

KEY (CORRECT ANSWERS)

1. D	11. C	21. D	31. D	41. C
2. C	12. C	22. B	32. A	42. D
3. B	13. A	23. C	33. B	43. D
4. C	14. D	24. B	34. D	44. D
5. C	15. A	25. B	35. B	45. A
6. A	16. C	26. B	36. B	46. B
7. B	17. B	27. C	37. B	47. B
8. A	18. A	28. A	38. A	48. C
9. A	19. D	29. B	39. A	49. B
10. D	20. C	30. D	40. C	50. C

SOLUTIONS TO PROBLEMS

1. $53,632 + 27,403 + 98,765 + 75,424 = 255,224$

2. $76,342 + 49,050 + 21,206 + 59,989 = 206,587$

3. $\$452.13 + \$963.83 + \$621.25 = \$2037.21$

4. $36,392 + 42,156 + 98,765 = 177,313$

5. $40,125 + 87,123 + 24,689 = 151,937$

6. $2379 + 4015 + 6521 + 9986 = 22901$

7. $50,962 - 36,197 = 14,765$

8. $90,000 - 31,928 = 58,072$

9. $63,764 - 21,548 = 42,216$

10. $\$9605.13 - \$2715.96 = \$6889.17$

11. $76,421 - 73,101 = 3320$

12. $\$8.25 - \$6.50 = \$1.75$

13. $(563)(.50) = 281.50$

14. $(.35)(1045) = 365.75$

15. $(25)(2513) = 62,825$

16. $(423)(.01) = 4.23$

17. $(6.70)(3.2) = 21.44$

18. $(630)(517) = 325,710$

19. $(35)(846) = 29,610$

20. $(823)(.05) = 41.15$

21. $(1690)(.10) = 169$

22. $2765 \div 35 = 79$

23. $\$18.55 - \$6.80 = \$11.75$

24. $2.75 + 4.50 + 3.60 = 10.85$

25. $9.63 + 11.21 + 17.25 = 38.09$

26. $112.0 + 16.9 + 3.84 = 132.74$

27. $65 + (14)(13) = 247$

28. $\$391.55 - \$273.45 = \$118.10$

29. $2016 + 1634 - 119 = 3531$

30. $\$367.20 + \$510.00 + \$402.80 = \$1280.00$

31. $(35)(65)(15) = 34,125$

32. $(40)(65)(10) = 26,000$

33. $(43)(.50) + (26)(.25) + (71)(.10) = \$35.10$

34. $(132)(.25) + (97)(.10) + (220)(.05) = \$53.70$

35. $(40)(.25) + (40)(.10) + (20)(.05) = \$15.00$

36. $\$29.61 + \$101.53 + \$943.64 = \$1074.78$

37. $\$132.25 + \$85.63 + \$7056.44 = \$7274.32$

38. $4010 + 1271 + 23 + 838 = 6142$

39. $(3)(\$20) + (5)(\$10) + (13)(\$5) + (43)(\$1) + \$218.00$

40. $(8)(\$20) + (13)(\$10) + (27)(\$5) + (3)(\$2) + (43)(\$1) = \$474.00$

41. $(6)(\$20) + (8)(\$10) + (19)(\$5) + (37)(\$1) = \$332.00$

42. $(13)(\$20) + (17)(\$10) + (24)(\$5) + (7)(\$2) + (55)(\$1) = \$619.00$

43. $(7)(.50) + (9)(.25) + (23)(.10) + (17)(.05) = \$8.90$

44. $(3)(\$1) + (3)(.50) + (7)(.25) + (13)(.10) + (27)(.05) = \$8.90$

45. $(73)(.25) = \$18.25$

46. $(173)(.05) = \$8.65$

47. The missing tickets are numbered 13,384 through 13,832. This represents $13,832 - 13,384 + 1 = 449$ tickets.

48. $2322 - 1315 + 1704 = 2711$ tickets left.

49. $273 + 342 + 159 - 217 = 557$ tickets left

50. $27,154 - 27,069 + 1 = 86$ tickets

ARITHMETICAL REASONING
EXAMINATION SECTION
TEST 1

DIRECTIONS: Each question or incomplete statement is followed by
several suggested answers or completions. Select the
one that BEST answers the question or completes the
statement. *PRINT THE LETTER OF THE CORRECT ANSWER IN
THE SPACE AT THE RIGHT.*

1. Traffic Enforcement Agents begin their daily patrol by   1.___
    taking at least 75 new blank summonses out into the field
    with them. However, agents may issue more or less than
    75 summonses per day. Below is a list of the number of
    summonses Agent Wilson took out into the field with him
    at the start of his patrol and the number of summonses
    he had issued by the end of his patrol.

	Blank Summonses	Summonses Issued
Day	At Start of Patrol	By the End of Patrol
Monday	75	65
Tuesday	75	70
Wednesday	100	90

Agent Wilson needs to know the total number of summonses
he has left, that is, the total number of summonses he
has not issued, following his Monday-Wednesday patrol.
Which one of the following formulas should he use?
   A. (65+70+90) - (75+75+100)
   B. (75+65) - (75+70) - (100+90)
   C. (75+75+100) - (65+70+90)
   D. (75-65) + (75-70) + (100+90)

2. Traffic Enforcement Agent Jackson begins his patrol with   2.___
    3 packages of summonses. Each package contains 25
    summonses. At the end of the work day, Agent Jackson
    returns with 1 package of summonses.
    How many summonses did he issue?
       A. 25   B. 35   C. 50   D. 75

3. Traffic Enforcement Agent Phillips began his day with   3.___
    5 packages of unused summonses. Each package contains
    25 summonses. At the end of the day, Agent Phillips
    has 9 unused summonses. Agent Phillips has to tell his
    supervisor how many summonses he used that day.
    Which one of the following formulas should Agent Phillips
    use to calculate how many summonses he issued?
       A. (25-9) x 5   B. (5x25) - 9
       C. (25-9)/5   D. (5x25) + 9

4. Six employees drive six passenger cars with Transit   4.___
    Authority decals into the Jamaica Yard parking lot after
    displaying their passes to the Agent. An hour later,
    two of those employees drive two of the cars out of the
    lot. Ten minutes later, two of those employees leave in
    one of the cars. A half hour after that, the other two
    employees leave in one of the cars with three other
    employees seated in the back.
    How many of the six cars that entered together remain
    in the lot?
        A. 1   B. 2   C. 3   D. 4

Questions 5-9.

DIRECTIONS: Questions 5 through 9 are to be answered on the basis
              of the following information.

    The Classon City Bridge and Tunnel Authority requires that all
officers collect tolls when on duty. Toll collection is an
important part of the job, and all transactions should be accurate.

5. A car with a trailer attached to it arrives at the toll   5.___
    booth of Officer Anderson. Officer Anderson tells the
    driver that the toll for this vehicle and trailer is
    $1.40. The driver hands Officer Anderson a $5.00 bill.
    How much change should Officer Anderson return to the
    driver?
        A. $3.40   B. $3.50   C. $3.60   D. $3.70

6. Mr. Eric Knoll arrives at the toll booth of Officer   6.___
    Piton. The correct toll for his vehicle is $3.85.
    Knoll mistakenly gives Officer Piton $2.55.
    Officer Piton should collect an additional
        A. $1.15   B. $1.30   C. $1.35   D. $1.65

7. A truck driver comes into the lane of Officer Enid. The   7.___
    toll for his vehicle is $2.85. He informs Officer Enid
    that he also wants to pay for the truck immediately
    behind his. The toll for the second truck is also $2.85.
    If the truck driver paid for both vehicles, the CORRECT
    change from a $20.00 bill would be
        A. $14.30   B. $14.45   C. $14.60   D. $15.30

8. A funeral procession of 8 cars approaches Officer Bragg's 8.___
    lane. The driver of the lead car asks Officer Bragg to
    charge him for all 8 cars. The toll for each individual
    car is $.75.
    How much change should Officer Bragg return after
    receiving a $10.00 bill?
        A. $2.00   B. $3.80   C. $4.00   D. $4.50

9. A truck driver approaches Officer Kendall's lane. The toll for the truck is $7.20. After the driver hands Officer Kendall a $10.00 bill, he drives away, forgetting his change.
How much change should the driver have received?
    A. $1.80   B. $2.20   C. $2.60   D. $2.80

9.___

10. How much change should a motorist receive from a $20.00 bill if his toll for using a tunnel is $2.65?
    A. $16.35   B. $16.65   C. $17.25   D. $17.35

10.___

11. On certain days, there are motorists who fail to pay the appropriate toll. On one day, this occurred four times. The unpaid tolls consisted of one for $2.15, two for $3.70 each, and another for $4.10.
The TOTAL amount of tolls not paid was
    A. $9.95   B. $13.15   C. $13.65   D. $13.85

11.___

12. While assigned to Toll Lane 3, Bridge and Tunnel Officer Johnson sees a convoy of military vehicles approaching the toll plaza. Capt. Hernandez, the driver of the first vehicle, tells Officer Johnson that he will pay for all of the vehicles in the convoy. Capt. Hernandez gives Officer Johnson the following for payment of the toll:
    2 prepaid tickets at $2.00 each
    3 prepaid tickets at $3.75 each
    1 $50.00 bill
Which one of the following methods should Officer Johnson use to determine how much payment he was given?
    A. Multiply the two tickets by $2.00, then multiply the three tickets by $3.75, then add those amounts to $50.00
    B. Add the number of tickets and bills, then add the two ticket amounts, then multiply the two amounts, then add $50.00
    C. Multiply one by $2.00, then multiply two by $3.75, then multiply three by $50.00, then add the three amounts
    D. Multiply the two tickets by $2.00, then multiply the three tickets by $3.75, then add the sums

12.___

13. Bridge and Tunnel Officer Storm is collecting tolls in Lane 7 of the Miller Bridge. A group of vehicles arrive in his lane in a single line. The driver of the first vehicle hands the following list to Officer Storm:
2 cars - Class 1; 3 vans - Class 2; 1 truck - Class 4; 2 cars with trailers - Class 5.

Vehicle Class	Toll Amount
1	$1.00
2	$1.50
4	$2.25
5	$3.00

In order for Officer Storm to determine the CORRECT toll amount to collect from the driver, he should
    A. add the number of vehicles in each class to the toll amount for the class, then add the four amounts together

13.___

   B. add the number of vehicles, then add the amounts of
      toll per class, then multiply the two amounts
      together
   C. multiply one x $1.00, then multiply two x $1.50,
      then multiply four x $2.25, then multiply five x
      $3.00, then add the four amounts together
   D. multiply two x $1.00, then multiply three x $1.50,
      then multiply one x $2.25, then multiply two x
      $3.00, then add those amounts

Questions 14-18.

DIRECTIONS: Questions 14 through 18 are to be answered SOLELY on
              the basis of the following information.

     Bridge and Tunnel Officers must calculate the correct change
to return to a motorist.

     Assume that the toll for each vehicle is $1.75. Determine
the correct amount of change that should be returned to the driver
for the following transactions.

14.   A $20.00 bill is given to pay the toll for one vehicle.   14.___
      The change returned should be
         A. $18.25   B. $18.75   C. $19.25   D. $19.75

15.   A $20.00 bill is given to pay the toll for three vehicles.   15.___
      The change returned should be
         A. $14.75   B. $15.25   C. $15.75   D. $18.25

16.   A $5.00 bill is given to pay the toll for one vehicle.   16.___
      The change returned should be
         A. $2.50   B. $2.75   C. $3.00   D. $3.25

17.   A $50.00 bill is given to pay the toll for ten vehicles.   17.___
      The change returned should be
         A. $25.00   B. $30.50   C. $32.50   D. $42.50

18.   A $10.00 bill is given for payment of toll for six   18.___
      vehicles.
      The Bridge and Tunnel Officer should NEXT
         A. return $6.50 to the driver
         B. return $1.75 to the driver
         C. ask the driver for an additional fifty cents
         D. allow the vehicles to go through since the toll is
            paid in full

Questions 19-20.

DIRECTIONS: Questions 19 and 20 are to be answered SOLELY on the basis of the following information.

Bridge and Tunnel Officers are required to sell rolls of tokens.

19.   Bridge and Tunnel Officer Victor began collecting tolls at 7:00 A.M. with 50 rolls of tokens. During his tour, Officer Victor was issued 25 additional rolls of tokens three times. When Officer Victor completed his toll collecting assignment, he returned 13 rolls of tokens. How many rolls of tokens did Officer Victor sell?
    A. 62   B. 112   C. 137   D. 138
                                     19.___

20.   Bridge and Tunnel Officer Smith was issued 100 rolls of tokens at the start of her toll collecting assignment. During her tour, she was given an additional 30 rolls of tokens. Officer Smith sold a total of 93 rolls of tokens.
How many rolls of tokens did Officer Smith have at the end of her tour?
    A. 7   B. 34   C. 37   D. 39
                                     20.___

KEY (CORRECT ANSWERS)

1. C		11. C	
2. C		12. A	
3. B		13. D	
4. B		14. A	
5. C		15. A	
6. B		16. D	
7. A		17. C	
8. C		18. C	
9. D		19. B	
10. D		20. C	

SOLUTIONS TO PROBLEMS

1. Number of summonses left = (75+75+100) - (65+70+90), which is 25.

2. (3-1)(25) = 50 summonses

3. (5x25) - 9 = 116 summonses were issued

4. 6 - 2 - 1 - 1 = 2 cars remain in the lot

5. $5.00 - $1.40 = $3.60 change

6. $3.85 - $2.55 = $1.30 owed

7. $20.00 - (2)($2.85) = $14.30 change

8. $10.00 - (8)(.75) = $4.00 change

9. $10.00 - $7.20 = $2.80 change

10. $20.00 - $2.65 = $17.35 change

11. Unpaid amount = $2.15 + (2)($3.70) + $4.10 = $13.65

12. Payment = (2)($2.00) + (3)($3.75) + $50.00, which is $65.25

13. Toll amount = (2)($1.00) + (3)($1.50) + (1)($2.25) + (2)($3.00), which is $14.75

14. $20.00 - $1.75 = $18.25 change

15. $20.00 - (3)($1.75) = $14.75 change

16. $5.00 - $1.75 = $3.25 change

17. $50.00 - (10)($1.75) = $32.50 change

18. Since (6)($1.75) = $10.50, the driver needs to pay an additional fifty cents.

19. 50 + (3)(25) - 13 = 112 rolls of tokens sold

20. 100 + 30 - 93 = 37 rolls of tokens left

TEST 2

1. The operator of a Transit Authority van hands Protection Agent Johnson a Material Pass listing the following: 31 boxes of No. 10 letter envelopes, 11 boxes - each containing 24 bottles of correction fluid, 18 packages of 14-inch photocopy paper, 12 packages of 11-inch photocopy paper, and 10 packages of paper towels. Agent Johnson counts the boxes and packages and finds a total of 79.
How many boxes or packages are missing?
   A. 2   B. 3   C. 4   D. 5   1.___

2. If a turnstile counter shows 28,841 at 10:00 P.M., and 1,348 passengers passed through that turnstile between 4:00 P.M. and 10:00 P.M., what was the reading at 4:00 P.M.?
   A. 27,303   B. 27,393   C. 27,403   D. 27,493   2.___

3. If a turnstile counter shows 49,739 at 11:00 A.M., and 2,157 passengers pass through that turnstile during the next three hours, what will be the reading at 2:00 P.M.?
   A. 41,896   B. 51,887   C. 51,896   D. 51,897   3.___

4. A squad of patrolmen assigned to enforce a new parking regulation in a particular area issued tag summonses on a particular day as follows: four patrolmen issued 16 summonses each; three issued 19 each; one issued 22; seven issued 25 each; eleven issued 28 each; ten issued 30 each; two issued 36 each; one issued 41; and three issued 45 each.
The average number of summonses issued by a member of this squad was MOST NEARLY
   A. 6.2   B. 17.2   C. 21.0   D. 27.9   4.___

5. A water storage tank is 75 feet long and 30 feet wide and has a depth of 6½ feet. Each cubic foot of the tank holds 9½ gallons.
The TOTAL capacity of the tank is _____ gallons.
   A. 73,125½   B. 131,625   C. 138,937½   D. 146,250   5.___

6. The price of admission to a PAL entertainment was $.25 each for adults and $.10 for children; the turnstile at the entrance showed that 358 persons entered and the gate receipts were $62.65.
The number of children who attended was
   A. 170   B. 175   C. 179   D. 183   6.___

7. A patrol car travels six times as fast as a bicycle.   7.___
   If the patrol car goes 168 miles in two hours less time
   than the bicycle requires to go 42 miles, their respec-
   tive rates of speed are _____ miles per hour.
   A. 36 and 6   B. 42 and 7   C. 63 and 10½   D. 126 and 21

8. The radiator of an automobile already contains six quarts   8.___
   of a 10% solution of alcohol.
   In order to make a mixture of 20% alcohol, it will be
   necessary to add _____ quarts of alcohol.
   A. 3/4   B. 1 3/4   C. 2½   D. 3

9. A man received an inheritance of $8,000 and wanted to   9.___
   invest it so that it would produce an annual income
   sufficient to pay his rent of $40 a month.
   In order to do this, he will have to receive interest or
   dividends at the rate of _____% per annum.
   A. 3   B. 4   C. 5 3/4   D. 6

10. If the price of a bus ticket varies directly as the   10.___
    mileage involved, and a ticket to travel 135 miles costs
    $2.97, a ticket for a 30 mile trip will cost
    A. $1.52   B. $1.34   C. $.66   D. $.22

11. A man owed a debt of $580. After a first payment of $10, 11.___
    he agreed to pay the balance by monthly payments in which
    each payment after this first would be $2 more than that
    of the preceding month.
    If no interest charge is made, he will have to make,
    including the first payment, a total of _____ monthly
    payments.
    A. 16   B. 20   C. 24   D. 28

12. The written test of a civil service examination has a   12.___
    weight of 30, the oral test a weight of 20, experience
    a weight of 20, and the physical test a weight of 30.
    A candidate received ratings of 76 on the written test,
    84 on the oral, and 80 for experience.
    In order to attain an average of 85 on the examination,
    his rating on the physical test must be
    A. 86   B. 90   C. 94   D. 98

13. A family has an income of $320 per month. It spends 22%   13.___
    of this amount for rent, 36% for food, 16% for clothing,
    and 12% for additional household expenses. After
    meeting these expenses, 50% of the balance is deposited
    in the bank.
    The amount deposited MONTHLY is
    A. $22.40   B. $36.60   C. $44.80   D. $52.00

14. Upon retirement last July, a patrolman bought a farm of 64 acres for $180 per acre. He made a down payment of $6,120 and agreed to pay the balance in installments of $75 a month commencing on August 1, 1983.
Disregarding interest, he will make his LAST payment on
   A. July 1989   B. August 1991
   C. January 1993   D. April 1996

14.___

15. 40% of those who commit a particular crime are subsequently arrested and convicted. 75% of those convicted receive sentences of 10 years or more.
Assuming that those arrested for the first time serve less than 10 years, the percentage of those committing this crime who receive sentences of ten years or more is MOST NEARLY
   A. 20%   B. 30%   C. 40%   D. 50%

15.___

16. Assume that in 1978 there were 21,580 vehicular highway accidents resulting in 713 deaths. This represents a 17% decrease over the year 1971.
If the year 1979 indicates a 6.5% decrease over 1971, the number of highway accidents taking place in 1979 is MOST NEARLY
   A. 23,846   B. 24,817   C. 24,310   D. 22,983

16.___

17. Of 35 patrolmen assigned to Precinct P,
     5 have 2 years of service,
     5 have 4 years of service,
     9 have 6 years of service,
     4 have 8 years of service,
     7 have 12 years of service, and
     5 have 16 years of service.
The average number of years of service in the Police Department for the 35 patrolmen is MOST NEARLY
   A. 6   B. 8   C. 7   D. 9

17.___

18. A patrolman purchases a two-family house for $31,800 and immediately rents one apartment to a tenant for $150 a month. At the end of two years, he sells the house for $35,200. Taxes, repairs, insurance, interest, and other expenses cost him $3,184.
His total gain from renting and selling, based on his original investment, is MOST NEARLY
   A. 6%   B. 8%   C. 10%   D. 12%

18.___

19. Precincts S, T, W, and Y are located in the county. The total number of patrolmen assigned to these precincts is 430. Precinct S has 7 patrolmen more than Precinct Y; Precinct T has 7 patrolmen less than Precinct Y; Precinct W has twice as many patrolmen as Precinct Y.
The number of patrolmen assigned to Precinct Y is MOST NEARLY
   A. 82   B. 86   C. 92   D. 96

19.___

20. Two radio patrol cars, coming from different directions,   20.____
    are rushing to the scene of a crime. The first car
    proceeds at the rate of 45 miles an hour and arrives
    there in 4 minutes. Although the second car travels a
    route which is longer by 3/4 of a mile, it arrives only
    1/2 minute later.
    The speed of the second patrol car, expressed in miles
    per hour, is MOST NEARLY
       A. 50   B. 55   C. 60   D. 65

KEY (CORRECT ANSWERS)

1. B		11. B	
2. D		12. D	
3. C		13. A	
4. D		14. A	
5. C		15. B	
6. C		16. C	
7. B		17. B	
8. A		18. D	
9. D		19. B	
10. C		20. A	

SOLUTIONS TO PROBLEMS

1. $31 + 11 + 18 + 12 + 10 - 79 = 3$ missing

2. $28,841 - 1348 = 27,493$ at 4:00 PM

3. $49,739 + 2157 = 51,896$ at 2:00 PM

4. Average number of summonses = $[(4)(16)+(3)(19)+(1)(22)+(7)(25)$
$+(11)(28)+(10)(30)+(2)(36)+(1)(41)+(3)(45)] \div 42 = 1174 \div 42$
≈ 27.95, closest to 27.9

5. Total capacity = $(75)(30)(6\frac{1}{2})(9\frac{1}{2}) = 138,937\frac{1}{2}$ gallons

6. Let x = number of children, 358-x = number of adults
Then, $.10x + (.25)(358-x) = \$62.65$. Solving, x = 179
(Note: there were also 179 adults)

7. Let x = rate of patrol car, $\frac{1}{6}x$ = rate of bike. Then,
$168/x + 2 = 42/\frac{1}{6}x$. Solving for x and $\frac{1}{6}x$, we get 42 and 7.

8. Originally, there are $(.10)(6) = .6$ qts. of alcohol and 5.4 qts. of water. Let x = added qts. of alcohol. Then, $(.6+x)/(6+x) = .20$. Simplifying, $.6 + x = 1.2 + .2x$. Solving, $x = 3/4$

9. $(\$40)(12) = \$480$. Then, $\$480/\$8000 = 6\%$

10. Cost = $(\$2.97)(\frac{30}{135}) = .66$

11. $\$10 + \$12 + \$14 + \ldots = \$580$. The formula for an arithmetic series is $S = \frac{n}{2}[2a+(n-1)d]$, where n = number of terms, a = 1st term, d = difference, S = sum. So, $\$580 = \frac{n}{2}[(2)(\$10)+(n-1)(\$2)]$. Simplifying, $n^2 + 9n - 580 = 0$. Solving, n = 20

12. Let x = score on the physical test. Then, $(76)(.30) + (84)(.20) + (80)(.20) + (x)(.30) = 85$. Solving, x = 98

13. $1 - .22 - .36 - .16 - .12 = .14$. Then, $(\frac{1}{2})(.14)(\$320) = \$22.40$ is deposited monthly.

14. $(64)(\$180) = \$11,520$. Then, $\$11,520 - \$6120 = \$5400$ to be paid in $75 monthly amounts. This would require $\$5400/\$75 = 72$ monthly payments. Since his first payment is August 1, 1983, his last one is July 1989.

15. $(.40)(.75) = 30\%$

16. Number of accidents in 1971 = 21,580 ÷ .83 = 26,000
    Then, number of accidents in 1979 = (26,000)(.935) = 24,310

17. Average = [(5)(2)+(5)(4)+(9)(6)+(4)(8)+(7)(12)+(5)(16)] ÷ 35
    = 8 years

18. ($150)(12)(2) + $35,200 - $31,800 - $3184 = $3816 gain.
    This represents $3816/$31,800 = 12%

19. Let x = number in Precinct Y, x+7 = number in Precinct S,
    x-7 = number in Precinct T, 2x = number in Precinct W.
    Then, 2x + x + x+7 + x-7 = 430.   Solving, x = 86

20. The distance traveled by 1st patrol car = $(45)(\frac{4}{60})$ = 3 miles.
    The 2nd patrol car travels $3\frac{3}{4}$ miles in 4½ minutes. The speed
    of the 2nd car, in mph, is $(3\frac{3}{4})(60/4\frac{1}{2})$ = 50

TEST 3

DIRECTIONS: Each question or incomplete statement is followed by several suggested answers or completions. Select the one that BEST answers the question or completes the statement. *PRINT THE LETTER OF THE CORRECT ANSWER IN THE SPACE AT THE RIGHT.*

1. A radio motor patrol car has to travel a distance of 15 miles in an emergency.
   If it does the first two-thirds of the distance at 40 m.p.h. and the last third at 60 m.p.h., the total number of minutes required for the entire run is MOST NEARLY
   A. 15   B. 20   C. 22½   D. 25   1.___

2. A patrol car had 11½ gallons of gasoline at the beginning of a trip of 196 miles and 5½ gallons at the end of the trip. During the trip, gasoline was bought for $10.85 at a cost of $1.55 per gallon.
   The average number of miles driven per gallon of gasoline is MOST NEARLY
   A. 14   B. 14.5   C. 15   D. 15.5   2.___

3. There are 15 patrolmen assigned to a certain operation. One-third earn $21,000 per year, three earn $22,050 per year, one earns $24,675 per year, and the rest earn $27,905 per year.
   The average annual salary of these patrolmen is MOST NEARLY
   A. $23,750   B. $24,000   C. $24,250   D. $24,500   3.___

4. In 1976, the cost of patrol car maintenance and repair was $2,500 more than in 1975, representing an increase of 10%.
   The cost of patrol car maintenance and repair in 1976 was MOST NEARLY
   A. $2,750   B. $22,500   C. $25,000   D. $27,500   4.___

5. A police precinct has an assigned strength of 180 men. Of this number, 25% are not available for duty due to illness, vacations, and other reasons. Of those who are available for duty, 1/3 are assigned outside of the precinct for special emergency duty.
   The ACTUAL available strength of the precinct in terms of men immediately available for precinct duty is
   A. 45   B. 60   C. 90   D. 135   5.___

6. Five police officers are taking target practice. The number of rounds fired by each and the percentage of perfect shots is as follows: 6.___

Officer	Rounds Fired	Perfect Shots
R	80	30%
S	70	40%
T	75	60%
U	92	25%
V	96	66 2/3%

The average number of perfect shots fired by them is
MOST NEARLY

    A. 30   B. 36   C. 42   D. 80

7. A dozen 5-gallon cans of paint weigh 494 pounds. Each can, when empty, weighs 3 pounds.
The weight of one gallon of paint is MOST NEARLY _____ lbs.

    A. 5   B. 6½   C. 7½   D. 8

    7.____

8. A radio motor patrol car finds it necessary to travel at 90 miles per hour for a period of 1 minute and 40 seconds. The number of miles which the car travels during this period is

    A. 1 5/6   B. 2   C. 2½   D. 3 3/4

    8.____

9. A parade is marching up an avenue for 60 city blocks. A sample count of the number of people watching the parade on one side of the street in the block is taken, first in a block near the end of the parade, and then in a block at the middle; the former count is 4000, the latter is 6000.
If the average for the entire parade is assumed to be the average of the two samples, then the estimated number of persons watching the entire parade is MOST NEARLY

    A. 240,000   B. 300,000   C. 480,000   D. 600,000

    9.____

10. Suppose that the revenue from parking meters in a city was 5% greater in 1982 than in 1981 and 2% less in 1983 than in 1982.
If the revenue in 1981 was $1,500,000, then the revenue in 1983 was

    A. $1,541,500   B. $1,542,000
    C. $1,542,500   D. $1,543,500

    10.____

11. A radio motor patrol car completes a ten mile trip in twenty minutes.
If it does one-half the distance at a speed of twenty miles an hour, its speed, in miles per hour, for the remainder of the distance must be

    A. 30   B. 40   C. 50   D. 60

    11.____

12. A public beach has two parking areas. Their capacities are in the ratio of two to one, and, on a certain day, are filled to 60% and 40% of capacity, respectively.
The entire parking facilities of the beach on that day are MOST NEARLY _____ filled.

    A. 38%   B. 43%   C. 48%   D. 53%

    12.____

13. While on foot patrol, a patrolman walks north for eleven blocks, turns around and walks south for six blocks, turns around and walks north for two blocks, then makes a right turn and walks one block.
In relation to his starting point, he is now _____ blocks away and facing _____.
    A. twenty; east   B. seven; east
    C. seven; west   D. nine; north

  13.___

14. A block has metered parking for 19 cars from 7 A.M. to 9 P.M. at a charge of 10 cents per hour.
Assuming that each car that is parked remains for a full hour and that on an average, for each hour of parking, there is a vacancy of five minutes for each meter, the amount of revenue from the meters for a day will be MOST NEARLY
    A. $10   B. $15   C. $20   D. $25

  14.___

15. The standard formula for the stopping distance of a car with all four wheels locked is:
$$S = \frac{V \text{ times } V}{30W}$$
where S is the stopping distance in feet, V the speed of the car in miles per hour at the moment the brakes are applied, and W is a number which depends on the friction between the tires and the road.
If the speed of a car is 50 miles per hour and W is equal to 5/3, the stopping distance will be MOST NEARLY _____ feet.
    A. 30   B. 40   C. 50   D. 60

  15.___

16. The radiator of a police car contains 20 quarts of a mixture consisting of 80% water and 20% antifreeze compound. Assume that you have been ordered to draw off some of the mixture and add pure antifreeze compound until the mixture is 75% water and 25% antifreeze compound. The number of quarts of the mixture which should be removed is MOST NEARLY
    A. 1   B. 3   C. 4   D. 5

  16.___

17. Assume that a parking space for six cars is to be outlined with white paint. The total area to be outlined is 24 feet by 40 feet, and the space for each car, also marked off by white lines, is to be 8 feet by 20 feet. The total length of white lines to be painted is MOST NEARLY _____ feet.
    A. 128   B. 156   C. 184   D. 232

  17.___

18. A police car is ordered to report to the scene of a crime 5 miles away.
If the car travels at an average rate of 40 miles per hour, the length of time it will take to reach its destination is MOST NEARLY _____ minutes.
    A. 3   B. 7   C. 10   D. 13

  18.___

19. During the first nine months of the year, an officer   19.___
    spent an average of $270 a month. In October and November,
    he spent an average of $315 a month. In December, he
    spent $385.
    His average monthly spending during the year was MOST NEARLY
        A. $254   B. $287   C. $323   D. $3,000

20. In 1995, there were 8,270 arrests in a certain city. The   20.___
    number of arrests increased by 12½% in 1996. In 1997,
    the number of arrests decreased 5% from the 1996 figures.
    The number of arrests in 1997 was MOST NEARLY
        A. 8,840   B. 9,770   C. 6,870   D. 7,600

21. Assume that parking space is to be provided for 25% of   21.___
    the tenants in a new housing development. The project
    will have five 6-story buildings, having seven tenants
    on each floor, and eight 11-story buildings, having eight
    tenants on each floor.
    The number of parking spaces needed is MOST NEARLY
        A. 215   B. 230   C. 700   D. 895

22. A stolen vehicle traveling at 60 miles per hour passes   22.___
    by a police car, which is standing still with the engine
    running. The police car immediately starts out in pur-
    suit, and one minute later, having covered a distance of
    half a mile, it reaches a speed of 90 miles per hour and
    continues at this speed.
    In how many minutes after the stolen vehicle passes the
    police car will the police car overtake it?
    _____ minute(s).
        A. 1   B. 1½   C. 2   D. 3

23. A police officer found his 42-hour work week was divided   23.___
    as follows: 1/6 of his time in investigating incidents
    on his patrol post, 1/2 of his time patrolling his post,
    and 1/8 of his time in special traffic duty. The rest
    of his time was devoted to assignments at precinct
    headquarters.
    The percentage of his work week which was spent at pre-
    cinct headquarters is MOST NEARLY
        A. 10%   B. 15%   C. 20%   D. 25%

24. Last year, the Department of Sanitation towed away 8,430   24.___
    cars which were abandoned or illegally parked on city
    streets.
    If the value of the abandoned cars was $1,038,200 and
    that of the illegally parked cars was $6,234,800, then
    the average value of one of the towed-away cars was
    MOST NEARLY
        A. $400   B. $720   C. $860   D. $1,100

25. Two percent of all school children are problem children. 25.___
    Some 80% of these problem children become delinquents,
    and about 80% of the delinquent children become criminals.
    If the school population is 1,000,000 children, the
    number of this group who will eventually become criminals,
    according to this analysis, is
         A. 12,800   B. 1,280   C. 640   D. 128

KEY (CORRECT ANSWERS)

1. B
2. C
3. C
4. D
5. C

6. B
7. C
8. C
9. D
10. D

11. D
12. D
13. B
14. D
15. C

16. A
17. D
18. B
19. B
20. A

21. B
22. C
23. C
24. C
25. A

SOLUTIONS TO PROBLEMS

1. $\frac{10}{40} + \frac{5}{60} = \frac{1}{3}$ hr. = 20 min.

2. Number of gallons used = $11\frac{1}{2} - 5\frac{1}{2} + \frac{\$10.85}{\$1.55} = 13$
   Average miles per gallon = 196 ÷ 13 ≈ 15

3. Average annual salary = [(5)($21,000)+(3)($22,050)+(1)($24,675)
   +(6)($27,905)] ÷ 15 = $24,217, closest to $24,250

4. Cost in 1975 = $2500 ÷ .10 = $25,000. Thus, the cost in 1976
   = $25,000 + $2500 = $27,500

5. 180 - (.25)(180) = 135. Then, $(135)(\frac{2}{3}) = 90$ immediately
   available

6. $[(80)(.30)+(70)(.40)+(75)(.60)+(92)(.25)+(96)(\frac{2}{3})]$ ÷ 5
   = 184 ÷ 5 = 36.8 ≈ 37

7. Each full can weighs 494 ÷ 12 = $41\frac{1}{6}$ lbs. Since an empty can
   weighs 3 lbs., 5 gallons of paint weighs $38\frac{1}{6}$ lbs. Thus,
   1 gallon weighs $38\frac{1}{6}$ ÷ 5 ≈ $7\frac{1}{2}$ lbs.

8. $(90)(1\frac{2}{3}/60) = 2\frac{1}{2}$ miles

9. Total estimate = (2)(5000)(60) = 600,000

10. Revenue in 1982 = ($1,500,000)(1.05) = $1,575,000
    Revenue in 1983 = ($1,575,000)(.98) = $1,543,500

11. 20 mi/hr means $\frac{5}{20} = \frac{1}{4}$ hr. = 15 min. to go 5 miles. Then, the
    car must go 5 miles in 20 - 15 = 5 min. This means 60 mph.

12. Let 2x = capacity of larger parking area, x = capacity of
    smaller area. Then, [(.60)(2x)+(.40)(x)] ÷ 3x = 1.6/3 ≈ 53%

13. He has walked 11 - 6 + 2 = 7 blocks north and is facing east.

14. There will be 13 hours of parking time at each meter, due to
    the 5 min. vacancy for each of the 14 hrs. of operation.
    Then, (13)(.10)(19) = $24.70 ≈ $25

15. $S = (50)(50)/(30)(\frac{5}{3}) = 50$ ft.

16. The original mixture has 16 qts. water and 4 qts. antifreeze. Drawing out x qts. means that the 20-x qts. mixture will contain 16-.8x qts. of water and 4-.2x qts. of antifreeze. Now add x qts. of pure antifreeze, so that now we have 4-.2x+x = 4+.8x qts. of antifreeze and 20-x+x = 20 qts. of the mixture. Finally, (4+.8x)/20 = .25. Solving, x = 1.25

17. Total length of white lines = (24')(3) + (40')(4) = 232 ft.

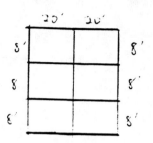

18. Time = $(5)(\frac{60}{40})$ = 7½ min., closest to 7 min. in selections.

19. Average = [($270)(9)+($315)(2)+(1)($385)] ÷ 12 ≈ $287

20. Number of arrests in 1997 = (8270)(1.125)(.95) ≈ 8840

21. Number of parking spaces = (.25)[(5)(6)(7)+(8)(11)(8)] ≈ 230

22. After 1 minute, the stolen car has traveled 1 mile, while the police car has traveled ½ mile. Let x = additional minutes required. Since the police car will travel ½ extra mile from the point at which it reaches 90 mph, (1 mi./min.)(x) = (1½ mi./min.)(x) - ½. Solving, x = 1. Total time = 2 min.

23. $1 - \frac{1}{6} - \frac{1}{2} - \frac{1}{8} = \frac{5}{24}$ ≈ 20%

24. Average value = ($6,234,800+$1,038,200) ÷ 8430 ≈ $860

25. (1,000,000)(.02)(.80)(.80) = 12,800 projected to be criminals

ANSWER SHEET

T NO. _____ PART _____ TITLE OF POSITION _____

(AS GIVEN IN EXAMINATION ANNOUNCEMENT - INCLUDE OPTION, IF ANY)

CE OF EXAMINATION _____ DATE _____

(CITY OR TOWN)   (STATE)

RATING

USE THE SPECIAL PENCIL.   MAKE GLOSSY BLACK MARKS.

#	A B C D E	#	A B C D E	#	A B C D E	#	A B C D E	#	A B C D E
1	:: :: :: :: ::	26	:: :: :: :: ::	51	:: :: :: :: ::	76	:: :: :: :: ::	101	:: :: :: :: ::
2	:: :: :: :: ::	27	:: :: :: :: ::	52	:: :: :: :: ::	77	:: :: :: :: ::	102	:: :: :: :: ::
3	:: :: :: :: ::	28	:: :: :: :: ::	53	:: :: :: :: ::	78	:: :: :: :: ::	103	:: :: :: :: ::
4	:: :: :: :: ::	29	:: :: :: :: ::	54	:: :: :: :: ::	79	:: :: :: :: ::	104	:: :: :: :: ::
5	:: :: :: :: ::	30	:: :: :: :: ::	55	:: :: :: :: ::	80	:: :: :: :: ::	105	:: :: :: :: ::
6	:: :: :: :: ::	31	:: :: :: :: ::	56	:: :: :: :: ::	81	:: :: :: :: ::	106	:: :: :: :: ::
7	:: :: :: :: ::	32	:: :: :: :: ::	57	:: :: :: :: ::	82	:: :: :: :: ::	107	:: :: :: :: ::
8	:: :: :: :: ::	33	:: :: :: :: ::	58	:: :: :: :: ::	83	:: :: :: :: ::	108	:: :: :: :: ::
9	:: :: :: :: ::	34	:: :: :: :: ::	59	:: :: :: :: ::	84	:: :: :: :: ::	109	:: :: :: :: ::
10	:: :: :: :: ::	35	:: :: :: :: ::	60	:: :: :: :: ::	85	:: :: :: :: ::	110	:: :: :: :: ::

Make only ONE mark for each answer.   Additional and stray marks may be
counted as mistakes.   In making corrections, erase errors COMPLETELY.

#	A B C D E	#	A B C D E	#	A B C D E	#	A B C D E	#	A B C D E
11	:: :: :: :: ::	36	:: :: :: :: ::	61	:: :: :: :: ::	86	:: :: :: :: ::	111	:: :: :: :: ::
12	:: :: :: :: ::	37	:: :: :: :: ::	62	:: :: :: :: ::	87	:: :: :: :: ::	112	:: :: :: :: ::
13	:: :: :: :: ::	38	:: :: :: :: ::	63	:: :: :: :: ::	88	:: :: :: :: ::	113	:: :: :: :: ::
14	:: :: :: :: ::	39	:: :: :: :: ::	64	:: :: :: :: ::	89	:: :: :: :: ::	114	:: :: :: :: ::
15	:: :: :: :: ::	40	:: :: :: :: ::	65	:: :: :: :: ::	90	:: :: :: :: ::	115	:: :: :: :: ::
16	:: :: :: :: ::	41	:: :: :: :: ::	66	:: :: :: :: ::	91	:: :: :: :: ::	116	:: :: :: :: ::
17	:: :: :: :: ::	42	:: :: :: :: ::	67	:: :: :: :: ::	92	:: :: :: :: ::	117	:: :: :: :: ::
18	:: :: :: :: ::	43	:: :: :: :: ::	68	:: :: :: :: ::	93	:: :: :: :: ::	118	:: :: :: :: ::
19	:: :: :: :: ::	44	:: :: :: :: ::	69	:: :: :: :: ::	94	:: :: :: :: ::	119	:: :: :: :: ::
20	:: :: :: :: ::	45	:: :: :: :: ::	70	:: :: :: :: ::	95	:: :: :: :: ::	120	:: :: :: :: ::
21	:: :: :: :: ::	46	:: :: :: :: ::	71	:: :: :: :: ::	96	:: :: :: :: ::	121	:: :: :: :: ::
22	:: :: :: :: ::	47	:: :: :: :: ::	72	:: :: :: :: ::	97	:: :: :: :: ::	122	:: :: :: :: ::
23	:: :: :: :: ::	48	:: :: :: :: ::	73	:: :: :: :: ::	98	:: :: :: :: ::	123	:: :: :: :: ::
24	:: :: :: :: ::	49	:: :: :: :: ::	74	:: :: :: :: ::	99	:: :: :: :: ::	124	:: :: :: :: ::
25	:: :: :: :: ::	50	:: :: :: :: ::	75	:: :: :: :: ::	100	:: :: :: :: ::	125	:: :: :: :: ::

ANSWER SHEET

TEST NO. _____ PART _____ TITLE OF POSITION _____
(AS GIVEN IN EXAMINATION ANNOUNCEMENT - INCLUDE OPTION, IF ANY)

PLACE OF EXAMINATION _____ DATE _____
(CITY OR TOWN)   (STATE)

RATING

USE THE SPECIAL PENCIL.   MAKE GLOSSY BLACK MARKS.

Make only ONE mark for each answer. Additional and stray marks may be counted as mistakes. In making corrections, erase errors COMPLETELY.